Visions of Paradise

Themes and Variations on the Garden

Photographs by Marina Schinz
Text by Susan Littlefield
with Marina Schinz

Stewart, Tabori & Chang, Inc.

New York

Page 1: A rustic shelter at Eyhorne is covered by rambling Kiftsgate roses (Rosa filipes)

Pages 2-3: The box-edged beds of Culpeper Flower Garden, situated on the soft slant of a hillside at Leeds Castle in Kent, are brimming with old-fashioned roses, true geraniums, campanulas, delphiniums, irises, and alchemillas.

Page 4: A pavilion at the Villa Marila near Lucca, Italy, opens onto the garden.

Page 7: The garden of the Frick Collection in New York was designed by Russel Page in 1975. A rectangular lily pond acts as the center of the garden, which is classical in feeling.

Text copyright © 1985 Susan Littlefield and Marina Schintz
Photographs copyright © 1985 Marina Schintz
Page 95: Courtesy of *House & Garden*; copyright © 1979,
Conde Nast Publications, Inc.

Published in 1985 and distributed in the U.S. by
Stewart, Tabori & Chang,
a division of U.S. Media Holdings, Inc.
575 Broadway, New York, New York 10012

Distributed in Canada by General Publishing Co. Ltd.
30 Lesmill Road, Don Mills, Ontario, Canada M3B 2T6.
Distributed in Australia and New Zealand by Peribo Pty Ltd.
58 Beaumont Road, Mount Kuring-gai, NSW 2080, Australia.
Distributed in all other territories by Grantham Book Services Ltd.
Isaac Newton Way, Alma Park Industrial Estate, Grantham,
Lincolnshire, NG31 9SD England.

Library of Congress Cataloging-in-Publication Data

Schintz, Marina.
    Visions of paradise.

    Includes index.
    1. Gardens—Design. 2. Gradens.
I. Littlefield, Susan. II. Title.
SB472.S356 1985   712'.6   85-2826
ISBN 0-942434-66-4

Printed in Japan
17   16   15   14   13   12   11

For Larry Rubin

Introduction

To create a garden is to search for a better world. In our effort to improve on nature, we are guided by a vision of paradise. Whether the result is a horticultural masterpiece or only a modest vegetable patch, it is based on the expectation of a glorious future. This hope for the future is at the heart of all gardening. Anyone who toils away at the soil must think a few weeks ahead or envision next year's garden, for most gardeners are convinced that improvement is on the way. Thus, gardening is an exercise in optimism. Sometimes, it is the triumph of hope over experience.

While all forms of gardening are worthwhile, not all results qualify as artistic achievement. If a garden is to be an aesthetic pleasure, a designing mind must plan the structure and choose the contents. As Russell Page pointed out, the idea, or theme, should come first. This theme can be anything: a geometric pattern; a group of plants; an existing feature of the landscape, such as a tree, a wall, or a body of water; or an architectural concept, such as a series of enclosures. If this theme is enhanced and carried out successfully—if the idea is clear; if the composition of volume, shape, and color is effective; if the planting is a harmonious whole—the garden can be said to be art. While basic gardening —making things grow—is easy, creating a masterpiece is more difficult. Many factors play a role. The soil, climate, timing, and availability of labor should be taken into consideration. Gardens are never finished. They are always in a state of flux, and their moment of perfection is ephemeral. To capture this vision on film is to fix that brief moment of splendor.

As a photographer, I am most interested in gardens that are visually satisfying. For this book, I have selected gardens of distinct character and spirit. I chose them for their clarity of style. They either represent the efforts of an individual gardener or reflect the approach of an entire nation. The individual gardeners included range from the cottage gardener, with a small, useful plot and a refreshingly naïve approach, to the herbalist, with a thorough knowledge of a specific group of plants. Some gardens celebrate the passion for a single flower, the rose, and the theatrical stage built to show off its supreme performance in June. The kitchen garden can be decorative as well as functional, while the perennial border may satisfy the painterly desire for color. Renaissance Italians taught us how to create delectable outdoor living spaces, while the French gave us classical gardens that exemplify a proud subjugation of nature. But the undeniable glory of horticulture is the English garden, whose basic structure of separate areas—its prominent feature—lends an air of expectation and surprise.

Today, we find our tastes tend toward gardens that are natural and uncontrived, loose and asymmetric. We have come to favor imperceptibly designed landscapes more than formal parterres. This predilection for natural settings is clearly a reaction to our industrial society. But since we have a knowledge of history as well, we try to preserve or re-create gardens of other eras—some precisely because they are not in harmony with our current ways of thinking, others because they are in tune with modern trends. Restorations of gardens from other periods—the Middle Ages, sixteenth-century France, and colonial America—fill in gaps that we sense and make statements about our own time and our responses to these horticultural styles. Our concept of paradise has changed through the ages, as has our attitude toward nature. The wilderness that was once our enemy has become a welcome friend, one that must be protected. In the world of horticulture, this means that a natural habitat now needs only a light botanical editing to be considered a garden. Nowadays, nature and climate, rather than the human hand, provide the variations. We have come to terms with bogs, woodlands, swamps, and deserts by transforming them into the gardens that bring us a little closer to paradise.

Marina Schinz 1985

Visions of Paradise

I

The Cottage Garden

Preceding page and above: Cottage gardens represent the oldest form of gardening, one that has been going on uninterrupted for hundreds of years. Eyhorne Manor in Kent is a genuine example of just such a garden. Roses, wisterias, and Virginia creepers climb up the walls of the fourteenth-century cottage, while true geraniums, poppies, foxgloves, and rose campions grow beside it in loose profusion.

Opposite, above: A mass of lupines, geraniums, lavender, and roses creates an unstudied appearance. Occasionally, Mrs. Sheila Simmons, the gardener, hybridizes a new rose.

Opposite, below: Herbs have their separate bed in front of the cottage. Pots are positioned to capture the sun or to be traded with visitors and neighbors. Chairs are casually placed in the midst of the flowery profusion, next to a yellow Phlomis fruticosa.

rofusion best describes the cottage garden—a place where flowers of assorted sizes, shapes, and colors spill over walls and paths, where herbs, vegetables, and berry bushes crowd among roses and fruit trees. The bloom is perpetual, as new blossoms draw attention away from any fading flowers. Planting is haphazard and cultivation is minimal, since the fullness of the beds makes it difficult for all but the most determined weeds to find a foothold. Seedlings are pampered in the beginning to assure a healthy start, and then allowed to grow freely. Plants thrive on this benign neglect.

Cottage gardens are usually attached to the unpretentious dwellings that line village streets and country lanes throughout the world. The oldest and most picturesque cottages are built of local stone, brick, or timber and covered with steeply pitched thatch roofs; simple surburban houses are the contemporary equivalent. Whatever its style, the house, which is often draped with honeysuckle and rambler roses, defines one edge of the garden; the other sides are enclosed by fences, stone walls, or hedges of hawthorn, yew, ilex, or privet. These create a protective shelter for a small, intimate space brimming with a remarkably varied collection of plants. The only set feature is a path that leads from the gate to the front door, which might be framed by a rose-covered arch or a pair of topiary peacocks.

A fine example of the classic English cottage garden is the one at Eyhorne Manor in Kent, which is squeezed between the low eaves of a timbered house and high privet hedges. The back door opens onto a patch of low-growing herbs and a bench nearby is laden with pots of

A cottage garden in North Devon with its neat rows of vegetables is enriched by a cluster of flowers near the road.

Opposite: The cottage garden at Sissinghurst is a somewhat stylized version of a typical cottager's plot. Its charm resides in its yellow, orange, red, and copper-colored flowers—columbines, geums, achilleas, roses, and dahlias among others. Four Irish yews surround the center area.

Overleaf: No cottage gardener leaves out flowers; in fact, some even specialize in a particular variety. A splendid stand of lupines occupies a considerable patch of this garden in Badminton. The back is reserved for vegetables and amenities such as a small greenhouse and a laundry line.

colorful geraniums brought out from the kitchen windowsill for the sunshine. Beyond the herbs, the garden's paths disappear into masses of flowers. Densely planted lupine, peach-leaved campanula, and coarse-looking phlomis carry their blossoms high; above them, climbing roses embellish an arbor and an apple tree, and cloak a simple shack that provides shade and sweet-scented shelter on summer days. Overall, the garden is unabashedly lush.

According to Margery Fish, one of this century's great cottage gardeners, the plants in a cottage garden are quite ordinary, "good tempered and pleasing," and not particular about soil or placement. There are ten classic cottage plants —white lilies, clove-scented pinks, honeysuckle, mignonette, roses, primroses, lavender, hollyhocks, hawthorn, and amaranthus. To these traditional plants, Mrs. Fish added rosemary and southernwood, which she liked to see flanking cottage doors; daisies, daffodils (both double and single), columbines, true geraniums, astrantias, and pelargoniums grown in pots. The majority of these plants are old-fashioned, which means that they have grown in cottage gardens for generations, but also suggests that they are straight species, with blossoms that are delicate in size, shade, and scent, unlike their gaudier offspring, the modern hybrids. Perennials and self-seeding biennials, such as foxglove and verbascum, are permanent elements of a garden; annuals are started anew each spring, grown from seed collected from the previous season's most attractive blooms.

The contemporary cottage garden has humble origins. The garden probably began as a medieval laborer's plot. On a small patch of

land, the laborer and his wife grew many things that were essential to everyday life: some herbs for making home-brewed medicine and others for adding to the soup kettle to enhance the flavor of vegetables and aging meats; fruit for preserving as jams and jellies; flowers for providing nectar for bees and fragrance for the house. The early cottagers were poor and could only afford to devote a limited amount of time and energy to their gardens. Traditionally, the cottage patch was the wife's domain: she tended the flowers and herbs, gathered plants from the wild, and traded with neighbors willing to swap coveted cuttings for handfuls of special seeds. Her husband assisted with the digging, pruning, and staking. Rabbits, chickens, and pigs were housed in the garden: prudent gardeners moved them around to enrich the soil, setting up portable wattle fences that prevented the animals from invading existing plantings.

In the early nineteenth century, as cottage industries increased, craftsmen and artisans took up cottage gardening. Since they were more prosperous than the laborers, their approach was somewhat more leisurely and their plantings more ornamental. Growing flowers became an avocation for the weavers, stockingers, and glove and lace makers who worked at home, where they had time to lavish special attention on the plants in their dooryard gardens. A weaver working near his window could spot a threatening cloud or a strong wind in plenty of time to protect his treasured plants or pull his pots indoors for safekeeping.

Eventually, some cottagers specialized in growing only certain strains of flowers. These people were known as florists, although

*R*oses spilling over doorways are a delightful feature of many cottage gardens.

*O*pposite: The hedges, or "bones," of this Devon garden are more than 300 years old. A true cottage garden, it is filled with hardy plants, including malvae, hollyhocks, feverfew, and santolinas, and is tended mostly on weekends.

*O*verleaf: This simple knot garden in Westonbirt village, Gloucestershire, is made of box. It probably dates from the Tudor period, when it would have been planted with lilies and pinks. Today, salvias and snapdragons predominate—these flowers were popular during the Victorian era. Thus, gardens often reflect different layers of styles.

*F*ollowing overleaf: The adjoining gardens in Westonbirt village show two contrasting styles. The garden in the background is divided into a vegetable patch and a flower garden. The one in the foreground, which also houses a Tudor knot, is composed exclusively of container plants. Pots are a prominent feature of cottage gardening, as is the barter of seeds and plants, and daily chats.

The only fixed feature in a cottage garden is a path leading from the gate to the front door. The one seen here is flanked by a type of lavender known as Munstead, which is named after Gertrude Jekyll's home. A darker variety of lavender bears the name Hidcote.

Opposite: Monet's flower garden at Giverny, the Clos Normand, is actually a network of cottage paths. In June, the main walk from the gate to the house is alive with roses, peonies, and campanulas, but in September, nasturtiums, sunflowers, and dahlias take their place.

they bear no relation to today's florists, and as prolific hybridizers they introduced many new varieties to the cottage garden. Anemones, auriculas, carnations, hyacinths, polyanthus, ranunculus, and tulips were among their specialties, and each species was painstakingly cultivated and crossed—so successfully that in one year more than 100 varieties of ranunculus were being cultivated in cottage plots. The florists revelled in competitive efforts to raise the perfect tulip or the most shimmering gold-laced polyanthus. They transformed the local flower show into a full-fledged English institution. Today, their spirit survives in the annual Chelsea Flower Show.

While the florists were prolific producers of new plants and used their gardens as laboratories, other cottagers were content to be passive collectors, harboring plants given to them by their neighbors and by the caretakers who tended the village's more fashionable gardens. The grounds around the manor houses nearby were a rich source of plants, for as tastes and styles changed, the wealthy landowners who could afford to discard their older plants did, and replaced them with popular new introductions. The cottagers were a receptive and far less fickle group: once a plant was happily established in their gardens, it was not likely to

Above: Monet delighted in planting masses of flowers, all of one color, such as these French marigolds in various sizes and shades.

Left: An elegant version of a cottage flowerpot is filled with pompom sunflowers.

Opposite: A cottagey mixture of annuals, perennials, and bulbs—cosmos, gladiolas, asters, dahlias, and marigolds—grows at Giverny in the style of Gertrude Jekyll.

Overleaf: Light colors prevailed in Monet's flowerbeds, as they do in his paintings. The planting was denser than his head gardener recommended—no bare soil was allowed to show, and successions of different flowers followed each other from spring to the end of summer. In June, roses, peonies, and bell flowers (campanulas) are all in full bloom.

be moved or replaced. Thus, the cottage garden served as a horticultural archive, where older species were collected and cared for.

Toward the end of the nineteenth century, educated people, worried about some of the effects of the Industrial Revolution, discovered that the traditional forms of craftsmanship and artistry, whose loss they were lamenting, were still being practiced by the lower classes. That finding sparked the Arts and Crafts Movement and revived enthusiasm for many household institutions, including the cottage garden. The cottagers' simple plots were praised by both practical and armchair gardeners for their selection of old-fashioned, hardy plants and for their loose, rambling look. Sophisticated gardeners, weary of the bold, overbred plants that nurseries offered, were delighted to find cottagers willing to share their flowers, and so these humble species made their way into grander gardens.

Around the turn of the century, as cottage gardening gathered momentum, gardeners divided their large gardens into a number of small compartments. These small compartments proved ideally suited to cottage gardens, which became a favorite theme. Vita Sackville-West's garden at Sissinghurst in Kent, for instance, looks to the cottage garden in its domestic scale and lush plantings, although it is a much more formal design. The compartment which she called her cottage garden includes a cottage, a wealth of flowers, and four Irish yews that surround a large central pot full of monkeyflowers. The symmetrical plan and carefully selected palette of reds, oranges, and yellows are evidence of Miss Sackville-West's artistry, and these aspects added a

*M*arie Antoinette commissioned Hubert Robert to design and construct a village for her in the park of Versailles. Le Hameau, an early example of "rustic chic," was built between 1783 and 1785. It consists of dairies, a fishery, a mill, and thatched cottages that were surrounded by vegetable patches.

*O*pposite, above: Marie Antoinette beheld this bucolic mill when she looked out the windows of her cottage. Below: The arbor at Le Hameau is made of iron hoops that are cloaked with Virginia creeper.

distinctly new dimension to the carefree character of the true cottage garden.

An equally artful rendition of the *jardin de curé*, as the cottage garden is known in France, is Monet's garden at Giverny. The Clos Normand section is a network of numerous paths, flanked by a colorful jumble of asters and daisies of all kinds, sedums, ageratum, nasturtiums, tremendous sunflowers, geraniums, and many others. The plants are grown in cottage style, with lush shoots and arching sprays everywhere. Standard rose trees give a dash of formality to the garden beds. Giverny is festooned with all sorts of climbers; but rather than keep them crowded against the house, Monet moved them into the garden. He adapted the rose-covered arch that framed the typical cottage garden gate, lining Giverny's primary paths and beds with iron hoops and rectangular trellises, draped with garlands of climbing roses, clematis, jasmine, and morning-glories. The look is exuberant, but the design of the garden is more controlled than that of an ordinary cottage plot.

More recently, Margery Fish took the opposite approach: in her books and in her garden, she championed the cottage garden's cause, defending its naïveté and lack of artifice. Her garden at East Lambrook was a mass of modest flowers. While not as dazzling as Sissinghurst or Giverny, this garden, with the plants she chose and the spirit that emanated from there, kept the simple cottage garden alive in the face of twentieth-century stylization. In fact, one of Margery Fish's lasting contributions was her inclination to focus on the beauty of individual plants rather than rely on the effect of masses grouped in bold blocks. She val-

*T*he driveway of this
California property is the modern equivalent
of the cottage path. Calendulas, snapdragons,
pentstemons, ranunculus, and pinks spill over
the retaining wall to greet the visitors.

*D*ay lilies and lythrum
are flowers originally gathered in the wild.
They are interspersed with daisies, bellflowers,
and cosmos in the cottage garden, which is the
front yard of John Howard Payne's home-
stead in East Hampton, Long Island. He
was the composer of "Home Sweet Home."

ued each plant for its unique personality, and that has proved to be a sound way to approach planning and planting a garden when space and labor are at a premium.

The cottage garden of today is not very different from the one found at the country dwelling of 200 years ago. Twentieth-century cottagers include both rural residents and city dwellers who can only escape to the country on weekends. The cottage garden appeals to them because of its simplicity and lack of pretension. Moreover, a number of useful and attractive plants can be grown in a small space that is not overwhelming to plan or taxing to tend. Enthusiastic plant collectors have the opportunity to plant whatever flowers, fruits, or vegetables strike their fancy, as anything can be included—space is the limiting factor, not style. In addition, the sense of enclosure typically achieved in cottage plots suits the modern gardener's need for privacy, and the loose, unrestrictive style stimulates both creative and horticultural instincts. That aspect, above all, endears the cottage style to contemporary gardeners from novice to expert; for cottage gardening is really an adopted attitude, and as such it can be applied anywhere.

The windmill behind John Howard Payne's home in East Hampton is framed by a meadow-like planting of cosmos, veronicas, bellflowers, and daisies.

Opposite: The path leading to Mr. Stanley Kunitz's front door in Provincetown, Massachusetts, is flanked by an abundance of densely planted stokesias, veronicas, balloonflowers, day lilies, phlox, and bee balm.

Above: The Chelsea Flower Show was conceived by country people who took pleasure and pride in growing flowers to decorate their vegetable gardens as well as their homes.

Below: Geraniums, or, more precisely, pelargoniums, were favored during the Victorian period, and still occupy a place close to the English heart. Today, many varieties are cultivated and displayed at flower shows.

Opposite: Growers and nurserymen have their own stands at the Chelsea Flower Show and vie with one another for gold medals.

II

The Herb Garden

Page 43: Henbane, or Hyoscyamus niger, *a poisonous plant among the medicinal herbs, was originally grown in the old physic's, or apothecary's, garden. For those interested in a theme, a garden composed of poisonous plants would be both an unusual and educational idea.*

Preceding overleaf: This medieval herb garden was established at the Bonnefont cloister at The Cloisters in New York in 1938. It is divided into different sections according to purpose—medicinal, culinary, aromatic, and other useful herbs, such as those needed to make dyes. Small wattle has been used to fence in each bed. Surrounding the well in the middle are four quince trees.

Opposite: Herbs are taken indoors for various purposes. Those that are not used in cooking or administered as old wives' cures can be dried or pressed for decorative purposes. Hanging are: Artemisia Silver King and wormwood, sage, bronze fennel, and Alchemilla mollis (flowers). In the mortar: borage flowers, garlic-chive flowers, and parsley. In the bottle: teucrium. On the bottom: leaves of bear's breeches, or Acanthus mollis, variegated sage, thyme, curly tansy, rue, hyssop (flower), and honeycomb. Honey was used to disguise the bitter taste of medicinal concoctions.

As a group, herbs are practical, decorative, and among the easiest plants to grow; just three or four of them will reward you with a bona fide herb garden that demands no special attention yet promises a bountiful harvest. They flourish without fertilizers, which only seem to dilute their pungency, and they repel potential pests with their natural oils. Herbs require minimal care yet provide almost immediate gratification —a feat few other plants can boast. They are grown for their leaves, and leaf production is not only plentiful but continual, beginning with springtime's early spikes of chives and extending through the last parsley harvested to garnish the Christmas turkey.

Furthermore, herbs are a rich and evocative group of plants, full of tales and traditions. They remind us not of pampered queens and courtiers, but of robust women whose gardens provided for family and household. From them—and from knowledgeable medieval clerics—we have learned that mint soothes upset stomachs, that tansy keeps ants away, and that costmary makes a useful bookmark. (Colonial women called costmary Bible leaf because they used its sharp, invigorating scent to keep themselves awake during lengthy sermons.) Such home remedies appeal to our curiosity about folk traditions and household lore. Today, herb gardeners are more likely to admire their sweet woodruff in the garden than to pick it for May wine; and they may not want to bundle their comfrey leaves into soothing poultices, but the fact that someone once did lends extra meaning and charm to growing herbs. This tradition is upheld by institutions like museums, botanical gardens, and historic houses, es-

pecially in the United States. The Cloisters in New York has an outstanding medieval herb garden; the Brooklyn Botanic Garden boasts an Elizabethan knot garden; and many reconstructions and restorations throughout the country feature colonial herb gardens.

The earliest herb gardens were physic gardens, which were set in the courtyards of medieval cloisters. These neatly patterned, simple, and functional plots were placed near the infirmaries, where they served as the medicine chests of the monasteries. To minimize confusion and reduce the risk of disastrous prescriptions, the monks grew a single type of plant in each bed and placed similar plants in adjacent lots.

This basic garden plan persisted for hundreds of years, until the end of the fifteenth century when the geometric layout of the medieval herb garden was abandoned. In an attempt to unveil the covert activities of his less loyal subjects, King Henry VII ordered that the protective walls of medieval castles be torn down—thus changing the face of the medieval garden, or *hortus conclusus*, by opening up the surrounding countryside. This decision had important horticultural consequences. Suddenly, there was room for larger, more ornamental gardens and a far greater assortment of plants.

During the sixteenth century, which was the heyday of herb growing, almost every cultivated plant was considered an herb, a plant of some value to man—either as food or medicine, as a dye for clothing or cosmetics, or as a potion to dispel devilish spirits. At this time, information about plants was collected and written down in many herbals. One of the best known, John Gerard's *Herball*, writ-

*T*eucrium lucidum *and* Santolina chamaecyparissus *make up the decorative strands of a Tudor knot. Black and white gravel is used to fill in the spaces between.*

*O*pposite: *The Elizabethan knot garden at the Brooklyn Botanic Garden is a reproduction of a sixteenth-century design. Knots were usually made of subshrubs or herbs such as rosemary, marjoram, myrtle, and lavender, which readily lend themselves to clipping.*

*O*verleaf: *Longacres, in Nashville, Tennessee, contains a walled herb garden reminiscent of the medieval* hortus conclusus. *Separate beds are set into the brick courtyard, and small sculptures of garden saints such as St. Fiacre and St. Francis are positioned on the wall to emphasize its medieval character. The tall flowers on the left are dill.*

Above: A stone seat in Sissinghurst's herb garden, a National Trust property, has a cushion of camomile (An-themis nobilis), which releases its scent when crushed. Although its medicinal value is questionable, that of the foxglove nearby is not. It yields the well-known heart drug, digitalis.

Left: Vita Sackville-West's thyme lawn at Sissinghurst consists of two rectangles planted with white and purple Thymus serpyllum, which blooms in July.

Opposite: The English herb garden at Alderley Grange, Gloucestershire, with its neat box-edged beds, combines a formal layout with a lush assortment of plants, very much in the spirit of the sixteenth century. Many more plants were considered herbs at that time than are today. The garden contains unusual flowers such as astrantia, henbane, and hemlock.

ten in 1597, had more than 2,000 entries. Yet the humble "sallet" plants were gradually moved from the herb garden to the vegetable patch, and peonies, roses, and the other showy flowers classified as herbs were given beds and borders of their own, leaving behind the greens and grays that we know as herbs.

To offset the removal of flowers to separate gardens, ingenious sixteenth-century herb fanciers created decorative knot gardens, with bands of contrasting plants, like boxwood, teucrium, and rosemary, woven into intricately brocaded patterns. The plants were neatly clipped and the empty spaces between the knotted strands were filled with herbs, flowers, or combinations of colored pebbles, crushed rock, and richly colored earth. In the most elegant knots, bits of ground glass were added for extra sparkle.

This tightly patterned Tudor tradition survives today in many American dooryard gardens, for it is the style that the first settlers brought with them from England. A number of colonialists arrived in Virginia and Massachusetts with John Parkinson's *Earthly Paradise* and Gerard's *Herball* and visions of tidy herb gardens laid out in formal beds; those gardeners who considered knot gardens too frivolous could still cling to the dictates of fashion by surrounding their herbs with low lines of trimmed box or winter savory. The eighteenth-century garden at Caprilands Herb Farm in Connecticut is Adelma Simmons' interpretation of what an early American herb garden would have looked like. Narrow paths, just one or two feet wide, run between the beds, thus allowing comfortable passage without dominating the garden design. A cen-

*M*asses of dill inhabit
the field adjacent to the building containing
the Herb and Seed Room at Hancock Shaker
Village, in Massachusetts. The Shakers com-
mitted themselves to self-sufficiency, and were
renowned for the excellence of their craftmanship
and agriculture.

tral bee skep adds height to what is otherwise a fairly flat plan, while small fruit trees and a picket fence define the perimeter.

Herb gardens have changed since colonial days. The herbs we now commonly cultivate for household use are parsleys, sages, rosemaries, and thymes, and as a group they share a number of similarities. Almost all are grown primarily for their leaves, which are strong in essential oils; and most are low in habit, since they lack the woody tissue needed to support long stems and branches. The most familiar garden herbs are an inbred group, related either by family or parallel evolution. Those that come from the same branches of the plant kingdom are similar in form: for example, the mints and sages, members of the Labiatae family, are upright growers with sturdy stems, opposite leaves, and lipped flowers; whereas parsley, dill, chervil, and angelica are members of the Umbellifera family, with feathery leaves and large, round clusters of flowers that resemble the blooms of Queen Anne's lace, their roadside cousin. Several other herbs, such as santolina and rosemary, are not related through ancestry, but through their place of origin. They are native to the Mediterranean region and have adjusted to hot sun and dry soil by developing a protective fuzziness or soft gray-green coloring.

These similarities make the herb garden a harmonious place. But to be more than a mere collection of plants, a herb garden demands something distinctive—a pattern, to provide structure on the ground; a theme to focus the gardener's selection of plants; or even a combination of the two. It should be set in a spot of its own, away from the dazzle of brightly colored flower beds—perhaps placed in a dooryard, or laid out in the center of an open lawn. A frame is more important than an enclosure, as fences and hedges are not necessary for protection; predators are put off by the strongly scented leaves. An enclosing hedge helps contain fragrance if it is high enough to buffer breezes, but that hardly seems necessary since herbs are generous with their essential oils. They release their scents freely, at the touch of a fingertip or the gentle brush of a passing foot.

As the need for home-grown herbs for kitchen and household pharmacopoeias has declined, the herb garden has become a more ornamental place. To pare down the selection of available plants, many gardeners begin with a theme: herbs for the soup pot, the salad bowl, or the linen closet, or those mentioned in the Bible, or included in Shakespeare's works. The most common herb garden is a culinary one, featuring parsley, chive, dill, basil, and others like chervil and tarragon. It is often set in a spot close to the kitchen and tends to be tidy, for most of the plants are compact even before they are pruned for the pot.

Not all herb gardens need be as well groomed as the culinary plot. For example, a garden designed to attract honey bees should have masses of blossoms. Usually, the bees stick to one type of flower as they gather pollen and thus they work most efficiently in gardens that are brimming with large clumps of vividly colored monardas, fragrant mints, and flowering thymes. The typical dyer's garden is an even looser collection of herbs. A plentiful harvest is indispensable in providing enough pigment to saturate homespuns and hand-loomed yarns, for a pound of

A room at Hancock Shaker Village is used for drying and packaging herbs, and reflects the sobriety and functionalism common to all the Shakers' working premises. Both their herbal medicines and seed business were successful commercial ventures.

Today, a dooryard garden in the United States may require the sacrificing of one's parking space. Mr. and Mrs. Dan Burton of Nashville, Tennessee, have done that in order to grow chervil, tarragon, parsley, and chive close to their kitchen.

Opposite, above: The tussie mussies, made of dried herbs by Adelma Simmons, are used for bridal dress rehearsals and are a reminder that herbs long ago had not only practical but also symbolic value. Thus a bouquet, depending on the herbs it contains, may be considered an expression of love, fertility, fidelity, or jealousy.

Opposite, below: The herb garden of the grand old dame of herbalists, Adelma Simmons at Caprilands, Connecticut, is divided into beds by beams, is graced by a beeskep, and is surrounded by a picket fence. The herb garden, which is basically a functional garden, has not changed very much in the United States since colonial days.

plants produces only enough dye to color a pound of wool. Goldenrod, sumac, milkweed, and dahlias all have a place in a dye garden.

Interest in herb gardens has been revived in recent times, although the number of herbs essential to the management of a contemporary household is few. Today's gardeners appreciate herbs for their decorative value—an attribute that had been neglected until the early days of this century. Inspired by the cottagers who had mixed flowers and herbs so freely, English gardeners borrowed the most striking herbs—the silvery artemisias, the big globe-flowering alliums, and soft green alchemillas—and set them in their flower borders. By doing so they opened the herb growers' eyes to the purely ornamental characteristics of their plants and introduced some handsome new members to the ranks of familiar herbs—plants such as bronze-leaved fennel, cranesbill, sedum, and euphorbia that once qualified as herbs but had been neglected because they were not familiar ingredients in the Tudor knot or in the classic *omelette aux fines herbes*. To the artistically inclined, gardening with herbs presents a chance to design with the forms, textures, and soft colors of the plants, for today's herb garden is a decorative place to display plants that may be useful, but are, above all, beautiful. John Parkinson summarized the combination perfectly in the 1620s: "Herbs," he wrote, "are for use and delight."

III

The Rose Garden

Old-fashioned roses are becoming popular once again. Above: Fantin-Latour, a Centifolia shrub; bottom: Albertine, a rambler.

Preceding page: The Roseraie de L'Hay-les-Roses, which is south of Paris in the Val de Marne, is the grandest of all French rose gardens. Created in 1894 by Jules Gravereaux, it is a formally treated garden that features more than 3,000 varieties of roses. The one in the foreground on the right is Sarabande.

In 1809, while France and Great Britain were at war, a ship carrying a pale pink rose was escorted safely across the English channel toward Calais. This precious cargo was Hume's Blush Tea-Scented China, a perpetual flowering rose that had recently come to England from China; and the recipient was none other than Josephine, Napoleon's wife and the Empress of France. She had a taste for luxury and a passion for flowers, particularly roses, which had developed during her childhood on the Caribbean island of Martinique. From her position at the pinnacle of French society, Josephine had the resources to indulge her floral fancies and the power to wield widespread influence. In the course of her lifetime, she transformed the rose from a plant of moderate appeal to a celebrated flower at the forefront of French horticultural fashion.

Josephine—whose middle name was Rose—was an ardent and extravagant collector, and like many trendsetters, she favored things that were foreign. She liked to import both her plants and her garden designers, and despite the war, her favorite source was England. In fact, Josephine managed to use the war to her advantage by staking claim to any horticultural bounty that French troops could plunder from British ships. Her garden at Malmaison—which was as unorthodox as her collecting methods —was one of the first to include a section devoted exclusively to roses, with square and circular beds set in winding grass paths that led to a rose-covered pergola. Each bed was thick with rose bushes, and some were accented with the choicest plants trained as standards. Josephine was also interested in developing new varieties and so en-

Hybrid Tea roses are unsurpassed for bouquets. In a vase, full-blown Fragrant Cloud fades gracefully. The first successful hybridization with the original China Tea Rose was performed by a South Carolinian named John Champney.

Overleaf: American Pillar, a summer-flowering rose introduced in 1902 and popular for a long time, is trained over a pergola at Bagatelle, the well-known rose garden in the Bois de Boulogne, Paris.

Verticality is of vital importance in a rose garden. At L'Hay-les-Roses, Paul's Scarlet and Mistress F. W. Flight so completely cover these tower-trellises that they look like pillars in bloom.

Opposite: The wall behind the statue on the Forum Romanum is casually adorned with roses.

couraged her gardeners to hybridize the many plants that she had collected. She made an inspired contribution to both horticulture and art by commissioning the artist Pierre Joseph Redouté to catalog the more than 700 roses in her collection. His paintings immortalized the flowers in her garden and her reputation as a superb rosarian.

Josephine's influence is still evident today, for roses retain their popularity, their separate place in the garden, and their French associations. For generations, the French have had a reputation as great rose breeders, and many of the best varieties have at least a trace of Gallic ancestry, with offspring bearing names such as General Jacqueminot, Amelie Gravereaux, or Cuisse de Nymphe.

The rose had been known to man long before Josephine's time, although its appeal had always been subjected to the tides of fashion. The Greeks cherished it as a symbol of love and beauty, and the Romans revered the flower so much that they imported roses from North Africa when they were out of season in Italy. For celebrations, the Romans wove them into garlands, crowns, and wreaths, and considerate hosts spread petals on the banquet floor, believing that the fragrance prevented drunkenness. Not surprisingly, the rose came to be associated with overindulgence. At one Roman banquet, several guests were suffocated by masses of rose petals that were dropped from the ceiling.

Unfortunately, such extravagances diminished the reputation and popularity of the rose. The flower was an anathema to early Christians, who were intent on disassociating themselves from everything reminiscent of the heathen Romans and their decadent festivi-

OB MERITVM CASTITATIS
PVDICITIAE ADO IN SACRIS
RELIGIONIBVSQVE
DOCTRINAE MIRABILIS
NV MAX
PONTIFICES VV CC
PRO MAG MACRINIO
SOSSIANO V C I M

ties. In general, however, their efforts to discredit the rose proved unsuccessful. By the Middle Ages, the flower crept back into Christian ritual, with the white rose representing the Virgin Mary and the red rose symbolizing the blood of Christ. Ultimately, roses permeated the very core of the Mass, in the form of rosary beads made from the fragrant paste of pulverized rose petals. In the secular world, the rose assumed a more decorative function. The white rose of York and the red rose of Lancaster were used as emblems during the War of Roses, and the Tudor rose later became the symbol of the British throne. In France, Madame de Pompadour used the rose as a more subtle signature and seldom appeared in public without one. In America, William Bradford brought bushes from England to plant in his Massachusetts garden; George Washington grew roses at Mount Vernon; and Thomas Jefferson set them in wild shrubbery at Monticello.

Besides being regarded as an object of beauty, the rose has long been valued for its useful properties. As the common name of the Apothecary's Rose (*Rosa gallica officinalis*) indicates, it was administered in its various forms to soothe all sorts of troubles, from headaches to hysteria, and was used in cosmetics, as well as medicinal preparations. Gerard and Culpeper, the herbalists, advocated its curative qualities, and twentieth-century research has proved that their recommendations were sound. Roses contain tannin, oil, wax, sugar, and several elements with astringent and anti-inflammatory properties; their hips, full of vitamin C, can be made into a syrup helpful in preventing scurvy. Extracts made from the flower's petals were often added to medicinal concoctions to improve their flavor and fragrance. Today, the rose's fragrance is still prized, particularly in the form of attar of roses, an essence extracted from the petals and used by the perfume industry.

The first roses to be planted in European gardens were brought from the Near East, and although they were a varied lot, these are now grouped together and referred to as "old-fashioned." Basically, these sturdy plants, which bloom once a year, in May or June, are hardy, disease-resistant, and deliciously fragrant. The oldest among them are the Gallica, the Cabbage, and the Centifolia roses. Another venerable group are the Damasks, best known for their heady fragrances. The Albas bear clusters of blooms, as do the Musks, which have a tendency to climb. The Moss roses are large-flowered shrubs, named for the threadlike glands on their stems and sepals, and the sweetbriars, or Eglantines, are prickly climbers with red hips that are almost as brilliant as their blooms. Among the hardiest of all the old-fashioned roses are the Rugosas, which have attractive fruit and a tough constitution.

In the early 1800s, just as Josephine was planning her garden, four new roses were introduced to European and American gardens. These were the China Teas, so named because of their place of origin and the fact that either they came on the ships of tea traders or their fragrance was redolent of the scent of fresh tea leaves. The four new roses created an instant sensation, for each had the delightful habit of flowering not once, but continuously. They had big blossoms, compared to the delicate old-fashioned roses, but they came with the disadvantage of being

Bagatelle, the charming rose garden in the Bois de Boulogne, was created in 1905 by J. C. N. Forestier. It is more intimate in character than the Roseraie de L'Hay-les-Roses, and contains cone-shaped yews and many rose standards, that is, roses grown as small trees.

Overleaf: Rose gardens rely almost entirely on trelliswork to give them height and structure. In the large "dôme" and pergola at L'Hay-les-Roses, roses are displayed by collections, botanically, historically, by origin, and so on. Leading up to the dôme is a decorative collection of large-blossomed roses.

Following overleaf: Roses have been known since ancient times. Here, a rose shrub at the Forum Romanum, where tales of the Romans' love for the rose still linger. Vergil and Ovid both sang of roses—even then widely cultivated.

Nine hundred species and hybrid roses, all labeled, form the Cranford Rose Garden at the Brooklyn Botanic Garden. A latticework pavilion overlooks the masses of roses, many of which are climbing up trellises or are trained on chains and arches. Buckwheat hulls used as mulch reduce the need for weeding in this otherwise high-maintenance garden.

tender and disease-prone. In an effort to combine hardiness and continuous bloom, the four —one of which was the plant that Josephine had arranged to have sent from England to Malmaison— were crossed with almost every available rose.

The four China studs generated an enormous family, and their offspring—referred to as hybrids—include innumerable combinations of color, size, and character. The most practical means of classifying the modern hybrids is in terms of hardiness. Those which tolerate the cold best are the Hybrid Moss roses, the Hybrid Spinosissimas, or Scotch roses, and the Hybrid Perpetuals—which, despite their name, produce nearly ninety percent of their flowers in June. Shrub roses are also able to survive winter weather without protection. Roses that are moderately cold-tolerant include the low-growing Polyanthas, the Portlands, the Floribundas, with their fragrant clusters of double flowers, their graceful kin the Grandifloras, and the renowned Hybrid Teas, which are a cross between the delicate China Teas and the hardy Hybrid Perpetuals. All of the roses in this group require protection where the winters are harsh and when dramatic changes in temperature threaten to damage plants with repeated freezing and thawing. Much to the chagrin of northern gardeners, the shrubby Bourbons, the Noisettes, and the true China Teas and their hybrids flourish only in mild climates.

By the nineteenth century, gardens devoted exclusively to roses were a familiar sight. Today, roses are the most versatile of all flowering plants, for there seems to be a rose to fill virtually every garden role. Tea roses and Hybrid Perpetuals make excellent bedding plants, with their elegant flowers and perpetual blooms, as do the profusely flowering Floribundas, Grandifloras, and Polyanthas. The large shrub roses can be used to enrich borders or provide background, while the spectacular bloomers can be trained as standards to highlight formal schemes. Climbers and ramblers covering arches, pergolas, trellises, and walls are the most desirable of all, as they provide the verticality that is essential to successful garden design.

To help focus attention above an otherwise flat expanse of blooming flower beds, gardeners often use verticals, and because roses resent shade and competition from tree roots, upright architectural elements are the most efficient way to incorporate them. The array of structures available for hoisting blossoms up high is as rich and varied as the flowers themselves. Pillars and towers become columns of clustered flowers by midsummer; scallops of rope or chain strung between uprights are like garlands, dripping colorful blooms into the beds below. Arches mark entries or points where paths intersect. Pergolas create tunnels of fragrant shade, and as strong linear elements, they can be comfortably used in the overall plan, marking main axes or dividing different sections of the garden.

Roses are best displayed against a uniformly dark, evenly textured background that offsets their flowers. Pliny set his rose bed in a ring of cypresses; countless gardeners since have achieved the same effect by surrounding their roses with hemlock, arborvitae, yew, or boxwood. An evergreen perimeter or a masonry wall will turn the rose garden into a separate area, which may not be considered an advan-

A modern cultivar climbs up a white latticework trellis.

*An updated version of a walled rose garden can be found at Penshurst Place in Kent. The formal beds are underplanted with rue (*Ruta graveolens*), which helps reduce the need for weeding.*

Opposite, above: A front yard in London has roses as its principal flowers. Delphiniums and other summer flowers are scattered throughout to create a more colorful effect.

Opposite, below: The arching sprays of Cornelia, a Hybrid Musk rose, with its warm pink blossoms and strong fragrance, is similar to many of the old-fashioned roses. When fully grown, it will reach six to eight feet.

tage when the flowers bloom in June, but it does keep the plants out of sight once they are past their prime. Although some roses have handsome foliage—*Rosa rubrifolia*, most notably, with its delicate gray leaves tinged with pink—and others bear colorful leaves and lustrous red hips in autumn, a non-flowering rose is not an attractive plant.

Most rose gardens tend to be formally designed, with geometrically shaped beds that create handsome patterns even when the roses within them are not at their best. The French have an affinity for formal design which may account for their outstanding rose gardens. Two of them are near Paris: L'Hay-les-Roses is an encyclopedia of rose growing, set up as a display garden with exhibits organized by both chronology and type. An allée records the entire history of the rose in flowers; a section of beds is devoted to the old roses that are no longer commercially available; and as if to balance that, another part of the garden has borders filled with the best of the contemporary French roses. L'Hay-les-Roses was developed in 1894 by Jules Gravereaux, an avid collector and thorough researcher. One of his horticultural accomplishments included reassembling the roses that Josephine had grown, which was a significant achievement, for her own garden had long since disappeared. He collected Josephine's roses in pairs —one set destined for Malmaison and the other for a Malmaison border at L'Hay-les-Roses.

Bagatelle, set in the Bois de Boulogne, is the other great French rose garden. It is stylishly structured by broad gravel paths and panels of turf that are edged with clipped box and sheared cones of yew. The layout is formal and green, providing a perfect frame-

A wall encloses the rose garden at Rousham House, Oxfordshire. Separate rose compartments ensure that the flowers are kept out of sight when they are not in bloom.

Opposite: The William Paca Garden in Annapolis, Maryland, is a restoration of an elegant pre-Revolutionary American garden. One of the four formal enclosures is designed as a rose garden, with old-fashioned roses of that period growing in beds edged with teucrium. In the center is a southern magnolia. The compartment in the back is a neatly clipped boxwood garden.

work for the roses that ramble everywhere—on pillars and posts, in beds, across ropes, and over arbors. Many are pruned as standards and set within the beds to enhance the formal plan; but most of the roses defy the geometric scheme with their profusion. A perimeter of massive old trees creates a dark, handsome frame, exaggerating the sense of the garden as a deep green bower dotted with masses of bloom.

An English rose garden presents an entirely different picture, most likely because English gardeners do not like to see bare earth, and therefore use underplanting, which is a recommended technique, provided that the accompanying plants do not interfere with the roses' roots. The subshrubs or suffruticose plants are often set beneath the roses, for as herbaceous perennials with woody lower branches, they are suitably scaled to stand up to the stems of roses. Subshrubs include many of the compact, low-growing herbs, from glossy-leaved teucriums to silvery cushions of artemisias. The grays and glaucous greens of herbs such as southernwood, santolina, and rue complement the warm hues of roses, as do the pale purples of lavender and nepeta, their traditional companions.

Underplanting ranges from the simple to the spectacular, depending on how intently the gardener wants to focus on the roses. Occasionally, English gardeners mix other flowers into their rose beds, perhaps delphinium for a vertical accent or true geranium for a splash of color. A rose garden is essentially an exclusive collection, however, and whether the addition of other blossoms enhances it is open to debate. Russell Page advised that gardeners choose a

Clockwise from upper left: A brick pergola graces the garden of the Villa Cimbrone in Ravello, Italy. A Lutyens-Jekyll pergola at Hestercombe is supported by stone pillars. Laburnum blossoms clothe this Chippendale pergola at the William Paca Garden, Annapolis. At Old Westbury gardens, blue wisteria complements a lovely turquoise gazebo and pergola.

theme, enhance it in every way possible, and eliminate everything that is distracting. If delphiniums don't draw a disproportionate amount of attention away from the roses, the combination is a comfortable one—but in general, in a rose garden, center stage is best reserved for roses.

Roses are available in almost every conceivable size and shape, as hybridizers continue to provide an ever-increasing choice of material. Most recently, breeders have created blossoms in colors other than the traditional reds and pinks. Contemporary nursery owners favor salmons and oranges, which perhaps is due to their professional appetite for novelty and botanical challenge rather than to their personal tastes. Because these sunset hues are difficult to use near other colors, they need a place of their own, if not an entirely separate garden, as such outstanding garden writers as Katherine White and Eleanor Perenyi have suggested. Hybridizers are equally determined to breed a blue rose, which is part of a trend toward color combinations that nature has managed to avoid, such as lime-green nicotianas, white marigolds, black tulips, and yellow sweet peas. In a more practical vein, breeders are constantly striving to produce a thornless rose, and at least one is already in existence. Zephrine Drouhin, introduced in 1868, is a perpetual flowering fragrant climber, and even with thorns, it would be worthy of a place in any garden.

Lately, rose growers have revived an interest in the old-fashioned roses, the species that were grown prior to the mid-ninteenth century. One of the staunchest supporters of these roses is Graham Stuart Thomas, an English plantsman who does not like to see roses in separate gardens, but prefers to use them as shrubs, in mixed plantings. He believes that since almost all of the older roses are larger, looser plants than their modern offspring, they demand an ample and informal spot in the garden. They work well with herbaceous perennials such as delphiniums, lilies, irises, and *Alchemilla mollis*. He is also an admirer of underplanting and of associating roses with white flowers, for white intensifies the classic rosy reds and pinks. Many of the old species and varieties flower only once a year, as do most garden shrubs. To Graham Stuart Thomas and the many people who are dedicated to the old roses, their full-blown blooms, soft colors, and exquisite fragrances are well worth the wait.

Growing roses is not for everyone, however. A well-groomed, tidy rose garden requires constant weeding, pruning, spraying, and cleaning. Roses are an ideal choice for those willing to invest extra effort for the promise of a brief but brilliant return. They are for the extravagant among us who like to gather their eggs in one basket, revelling in a June display that can best be compared to a firework display: spectacular and short-lived.

*P*ergolas were developed by the earliest gardeners, probably for the cultivation of grapes. In the flower world, they are most often used for roses, but are also used for other climbing plants. Roses are trained on a white-lattice trellis at Huntington Gardens, San Marino, California.

*O*verleaf: At the cloister of Santa Chiara Church in Naples, Italy, the four pergolas are made of majolica tiles, decorated with garlands of fruits and flowers, from nearby Capodimonte. They divide the courtyard into four rectangles, each one planted with flowers and vegetables and tended by monks.

IV

The Kitchen Garden

Petunias add a dash of color at the foot of clipped pear trees.

Preceding page: At first glance, a basketful of September crops may be thought to contain only native vegetables. In fact, the contents are likely to have come from all the corners of the globe. Eggplants originated in Asia, Savoy cabbage in Holland, beets in Germany, spinach in Persia, and radishes in China. Indigenous to the New World, however, are tomatoes, potatoes, peppers, squashes, corn, and green beans.

Opposite: The world's most delightful kitchen garden can be found at the Château de Villandry, which is owned by the Carvallo family. It is, in fact, a reconstruction of a sixteenth-century garden, laid out as a formal parterre and filled with vegetables available at that time, as well as some flowers. The garden has two peak seasons—June and September (shown here).

Known as the kitchen garden in England, the vegetable patch in America, l'orto in Italy, and le potager in France, this garden is an orderly plot of land on which gardeners have been growing vegetables since the beginning of agriculture. A kitchen garden can be as decorative as it is utilitarian, made into a refined place less by the choice of its plants than by its overall arrangement and by its meticulous execution. Order and tidiness are its foremost virtues, brought about by necessity and sound gardening practice. A proper kitchen garden contains not only the familiar garden fare—salad greens in low rows, tomatoes neatly staked, peas climbing tidy trellises, but also the more unusual crops, such as shallots, leeks, thin-skinned new potatoes, and sorrel, alongside herbs for household use and flowers for cutting. Fruit is planted as well, with raspberries and currants trained to hug the fence or wall, while apples or pears are either espaliered or grown upright in garden corners.

In terms of technique, planning a kitchen garden is a precise undertaking, ordered by a logical set of guidelines. It is the perfect garden for beginners and fastidious gardeners who like to work within a structural framework. Basic agricultural principles determine its layout as well as the rotation plans that spell out what plants should grow where in seasons to come. A fundamental feature of the classic kitchen garden is a wall, ideally a high one of stone or brick, which will protect the young crops from hungry foragers and from wind, will capture the warmth of the early spring sunshine, and will be able to support a collection of vines and espaliered fruit trees. Alternatively,

a fence or a hedge will provide the protective perimeter and conceal the garden during its less attractive phases. Plants are set in neat rows that are simple to sow and easy to cultivate, and they are evenly spaced so that each plant has ample room to spread. If beds are part of the plan, they are made just wide enough to allow the gardener room to reach for weeds. In the more decorative gardens, lines of low-growing boxwood edge the beds, or cordoned pears provide dappled shade that protects seedlings from midsummer heat; for those of a simpler design, borders of herbs or flowers serve the same purpose. Trellises are frequently used for peas, beans, tomatoes, squashes, and sometimes cucumbers to train them to grow vertically, so that they can soak up the sunshine and are easy to see and pick.

Paths play an important role in the kitchen garden. They should be paved or well-packed to provide firm, dry footing for wheel barrows and heavy boots. The central space made where the paths cross is often occupied by something functional. Wells and cisterns were common before garden hoses; the latter, although less familiar, were favored by many gardeners who preferred to pamper their tender plants with rainwater. Today, the cistern is often replaced by a small pool or perhaps a sundial.

One practical component of a kitchen garden is usually tucked away from view, sometimes behind a screen of blackberries. It is the compost pile, which converts this season's weeds and potato peels into rich black earth that will nourish new crops. Tender seedlings and cuttings are harbored in a cold frame nearby; they will make room for lettuces and salad herbs once frost settles over the garden. A de-

Above: Two of nine squares that contain vegetables of contrasting colors are planted in different patterns. The blues of leeks and cabbages, the greens of carrots and celery, and the reds of Swiss chard and beets are quite striking. Among the other vegetables planted here are chicory, zucchini, brussels sprouts, eggplants, pimentos, basil, parsley, and cherry tomatoes.

Below: Red-hearted cabbages (Lyssako) have considerable decorative appeal.

Opposite: Roses and cabbages dominate Villandry's potager. The cabbage is known as the king of vegetables, as the rose is considered the queen of flowers. Here, the cabbage is paid homage to in its ornamental form. White-hearted cabbages are grown in box-edged beds, punctuated by standard rose trees.

Overleaf: The magnificent kitchen garden of Upton House, a National Trust property in Warwickshire, enjoys a sunny and sheltered position below the mansion. It is bordered by brick walls, ancient yew hedges, and at the bottom by the banks of a lake.

Above: Although gooseberries were considered a choice fruit during the Victorian period, they are sadly reduced to unsatisfactory varieties in the United States. Devoted gardeners pinch off young fruits to make the remaining gooseberries grow to huge marble size.

Left: Every skilled gardener eventually attempts the tricky task of espaliering a fruit tree. The fan-shaped cherry tree benefits from the protection and stored warmth of the brick wall behind.

voted four-season gardener—the status that almost every kitchen gardener eventually aspires to—will conceal a hot bed in an unused corner of the garden, adjacent to an old foundation or wall, if possible, where layered compost and manure generate enough heat to coax melons and strawberries to bear fruit for the midwinter breakfast table.

Annual vegetables and flowers occupy most of the space in the typical kitchen garden. Perennial crops such as asparagus, rhubarb, sorrel, and some of the herbs are given permanent beds so that they can be left undisturbed from season to season. To insure a good head start in spring, early peas and lettuces are usually tucked into a sunny spot, and wanderers such as cucumbers and melons are set apart so as not to smother less expansive growers. Within the beds, it is important to keep in mind a few basic facts: east- and west-running rows get the most sunshine, and tall plants such as corn and pole-trained beans cast minimal shade if lined along the northern edge. Blackberries, currants, and gooseberries are conveniently grown in broad borders between the wall and a perimeter path, where they can bask in the sun and reflected heat. Cherry or pear trees are used to mark the garden's four corners, for they are relatively upright growers and create less shade than their widely branched alternatives, the apples and apricots.

Cropping is the technique that governs replanting once the early vegetables are harvested. According to Bernard McMahon, a widely read sage of nineteenth-century American gardening, "The great art in cropping a kitchen garden is to make the most of every part of the ground . . . by having each quar-

Clockwise from left: A robin has wisely chosen to build its nest in a berry garden. Butternut squashes are among the fruits native to the United States. Their male flowers can be eaten like those of their Italian cousin. Sweet peas, valued for their red, pink, white, and blue flowers, are often grown on trellises in vegetable gardens. New hybrids have bigger flowers, but they are less fragrant than the older varieties.

The layouts of Swiss peasant gardens in the Emmenthal have not changed much since the seventeenth century. Like Villandry, the garden consists of geometric vegetable beds bordered by clipped box hedges. Braided onions are hung on the balcony of the barn to dry.

ter well occupied with as many crops as possible." Grouping early and late harvests insures efficient use of time and space; sowing lettuces between seedling carrots and turnips doubles garden productivity, for the young leaves will be ready for the salad bowl long before they begin to cramp the roots below; and staggered sowing helps assure that every tomato doesn't ripen on the same sunny August day. Companion planting even suggests which plants will thrive as neighbors.

Surviving plans of medieval cloisters suggest that kitchen gardens were planted systematically, like the physic gardens; each rectangular bed filled with a different vegetable. Flowers and culinary herbs were part of the kitchen patch, for they were important ingredients in medieval cuisine, particularly in "sallets," which fifteenth-century gourmets considered somewhat exotic eating. Gradually, uncooked greens became fashionable fare; and by the seventeenth century, salads were considered one of the culinary treats of English society. In fact, King James II's head gardener believed that salads should contain no less than thirty-five different ingredients, including rosebuds, cowslips, daisies, violets, and saffron along with greens such as mustard, cress, corn-salad, and dandelions. Clearly, any kitchen gardener intent on keeping up with culinary fashion would have planted flowers among the peas and carrots.

The kitchen garden was originally located in the vicinity of the house. A developing sense of artistry, however, encouraged sophisticated gardeners to devote the prominent area near the mansion to flowers, and to relegate the less esteemed food crops to a peripheral site. In 1629, John Parkinson wrote: "The many different scents that arise from the herbs (such) as cabbages, onions, etc. are scarce well pleasing to perfume the lodgings of any house." By the eighteenth century, the kitchen garden was removed out of sight altogether and placed near the stables and the manure pile, so as not to intrude upon the carefully composed landscape scenes that had become so popular.

Some gentlemen farmers resisted the trend to disassociate the humble kitchen garden from the house; particularly those in colonial America, for whom practical constraints and convenience were far more pressing than aesthetic considerations. William Penn, Thomas Jefferson, and George Washington were all devoted kitchen gardeners. Mount Vernon's elaborate and extensive kitchen garden flanks the main entrance to the house, opposite a formal boxwood garden.

American interest in vegetables began through necessity when the first settlers arrived, and was greatly enhanced by the native vegetables they found: potatoes, sweet potatoes, green peppers, pumpkins, squashes, Jerusalem artichokes (known as Canadian potatoes), corn, even "French" beans. Moreover, early Americans were more receptive to the varieties of plants, as well as to some of the gardening techniques the native Indians showed them than were the Europeans, who clung to their old ways and whose acceptance of the potato, for instance, was only brought about by famine and armed Prussian soldiers.

Nowhere is vegetable gardening more avidly pursued than it is now in the United States, where gardeners appreciate the well-organized plan, logical planting,

A kitchen garden in Westchester County, New York, is based on a geometric design. Railway ties make practical substitutes in those climates where box hedges have not proved hardy. An electric wire strung on top of a fence and a stone wall keep out deer.

The rose-covered folly in the Duchess of Beaufort's former kitchen garden at Badminton was designed by Russell Page. He placed it in the center of a walled enclosure and used box to frame the beds.

and expert techniques that are involved. Utility contributes to the kitchen garden's appeal as well, for Americans are steeped in the values of Puritanism and self-sufficiency. Devoted vegetable growers are convinced that their time and energy are well-spent and constructively rewarded, although experience proves that from seed packet to salad, a homegrown tomato costs considerably more than a mass-produced one. Vegetables, however, are dependable plants, and that endears them to the practical-minded gardener. A brussel sprout seed burgeons and bears brussel sprouts; pumpkins swell in time for jack-o'lanterns and Thanksgiving pies; and turnips become flushed with purple just as the catalogs promise they will.

The quick results of growing vegetables suit Americans and their mobility well. Most food crops are annual, completing their growth cycles in relatively short seasons: a tiny seed becomes a tasty radish in just over three weeks; lettuces are ready for salads only fifty days after sowing; and in three months a few tomato plants produce an abundant crop. As a one-season endeavor, a kitchen patch satisfies the beginning gardener's desire for rapid rewards. Mistakes are of minor consequence because seeds are inexpensive and once planted, their cycles are quick. The first frost eliminates the season's fiascos, and by January the kitchen garden begins anew, at least in theory, as the gardener combs catalogs, carefully avoiding the crops that contributed more to the compost heap than to the kitchen.

Kitchen gardens have proved even more attractive in light of the rising demand for clean, tasty fruits and vegetables that have not been contaminated by chemicals. There

An ingeniously designed round vegetable and flower garden in Connecticut is watered by a single sprinkler hoisted on a tripod in the middle of the garden. Cages keep birds and predators away from the tomatoes.

Overleaf: In grander schemes, neatly kept vegetable and cutting gardens are frequently located on a peripheral site, as they are here, at Villar Perosa, Mr. and Mrs. Gianni Agnelli's mountain residence near Turin.

*A*bove: *Many English-women include some flowers in their kitchen gardens for purely decorative reasons. At Clovelly Court, in Devon, hollyhocks are planted next to cabbages.*

*B*elow left: *Rosemary Verey's vegetable garden, inspired by the one at Villandry, features roses and decorative cabbages.*

*B*elow right: *Portable cloches help speed up the growing process in Rosemary Verey's garden in Gloucestershire.*

is now a large market for organic gardening principles and publications. Rodale Press, in particular, has sold American gardeners on the virtues of composting, companion planting, and importing boxes full of praying mantises and ladybugs to feast on garden pests. Ruth Stout, a writer and confirmed New York City dweller until she was converted to the country in her mid-forties, was determined to have a bountiful vegetable garden without being a complete slave to it. Twenty-five years after she first tilled her garden, she had figured out how. She gathered her wisdom in a delightful book called *How to Have a Green Thumb Without an Aching Back*, and with it, opened like-minded Americans' eyes to the merits of mulching, that is, spreading a covering, usually of compost, peat, or straw, over the surface of soil to suppress weeds and conserve moisture.

Such practicalities are only part of the art of cultivating a kitchen garden, however. Sooner or later, every kitchen gardener seems to become a horticultural virtuoso. One chooses to grow only tomatoes—reds, yellows, and oranges, from the tiny cherries to plum and pear-shaped varieties; another concentrates on salads, choosing international lettuces such as *laitue grosse blonde paresseuse*, arugula from Italy, watercress, and French sorrel. Perhaps a more adventurous gardener will plant everything in odd colors: white eggplants, white strawberries, and white cucumbers; purple peas; yellow beets; blue potatoes and red lettuces. The flower fancier might specialize in vegetables with showy blossoms such as eggplant, okra, and scarlet runner beans; or with edible blooms such as nasturtium, calendula, chive, squash, and borage.

Above: Allotment gardens in or near towns and industrial areas, such as this one in Faversham, England, allow city dwellers to grow their favorite plants and flowers.

Right: A Korean woman and her son are ready to sow beans in an allotment garden in Santa Barbara, California.

*T*homas Jefferson's immense kitchen garden at Monticello contained more than 250 varieties of herbs and vegetables, including decorative beans and the symbol of American harvests, the pumpkin.

Thus the desire to push nature to her limits becomes part of the kitchen gardener's craft: producing the earliest peach; picking a tender head of garden lettuce on a cold January day; growing a globe artichoke when everyone who knows better insists that the nights are impossibly cold; and grafting a tree that will bear five different kinds of apples. Outside of the garden, competition between eager vegetable growers has been institutionalized, as it was in the days of the cottagers who entered their prime specimens in flower shows. No country fair would be complete without kitchen gardeners from eight to eighty proudly displaying their produce, hoping to reap an extra reward for the most monstrous pumpkin, the most perfect purple eggplant, or for creating the best bread-and-butter pickles and the tastiest blueberry pie.

Above: George Washington's kitchen garden at Mount Vernon is a classical example of an American vegetable garden. It is surrounded by brick walls with picket fences on top; two octagonal garden sheds punctuate the ends of the garden. Espaliered fruit is trained on the walls as low hedges, and vegetables, comparable to those available in the eighteenth century, are grown in geometric beds.

Right: The greenhouse designed by George Washington was completed in 1789. It houses baskets, tools, and cloches in summer and serves as a sheltered storage place for tender citrus trees and other semitropical plants in winter.

V

The Perennial Border

To create a full-fledged perennial border is perhaps the ultimate aesthetic achievement in garden design. It is an art as closely allied with painting as it is with horticultural expertise, for the goal in growing flowers is to compose a garden picture with form, texture, and carefully coordinated washes of color. In the garden, however, success is even more difficult to achieve, for flowers, once established, do not last. They fade and die, and a compatible group of later bloomers must be ready to take their place if the visual interest is to be maintained for any length of time. Furthermore, herbaceous perennials encompass a vast group of plants; thus the development of a perennial border is a personal pursuit, a matter not of rules, but of individual style and taste.

Perennials are basically field flowers, most at home in a situation that captures the breadth and sparkle of a midsummer meadow. Therefore, the quintessential border should look unstructured and informal, with drifts of flowers that recall their native habitat. But the casual appearance of the perennial border is carefree only to the eye. It is, in fact, one of the most complex garden features to plan, as it depends almost entirely on the short-lived effect of flowers. Pattern, which provides the theme for so many other types of gardens, plays little part here: flowers are the main attraction, gathered in gay or muted combinations that will bloom simultaneously and for as long as possible. The perennials that form the bulk of the border are hardy flowering plants, dying to the ground each winter, surviving from season to season. Nevertheless, the plants that go into the border need not be exclusively

perennial, entirely herbaceous, or absolutely hardy. Annuals, bulbs, and tender bedding plants can be relied on to contribute invaluable patches of color before or after the perennial flowers peak; shrubs can be added to give solidity and help divide the border into separate bays for special groups of plants or colors. Climbers can be used to enrich the back wall and small trees to supply height or accent, while evergreens and foliage plants can provide texture and interest when the flowers are not in full swing.

Whether the border is called perennial, herbaceous, or mixed, it will be at its most dazzling in the summer, as most perennials bloom between June and September. To stretch the blooming period is a difficult endeavor, and the foremost decision the discriminating gardener has to make before planning the border is whether to have some flowers in bloom throughout the growing season, which can give the border an unwanted, spotty appearance, or whether to concentrate on having all the blooms coincide, thus ensuring the brilliance of a finely tuned and synchronized display. If the latter approach is chosen, then the prime flowering period will occur either from spring to mid-season (July) or in late August and September.

The first step in creating a perennial border is the establishment of a solid, vertical background; this can be a brick or stone wall, a sheared yew hedge, or a tangle of rambling roses or shrubs. A flower border can also be set in an open lawn, in which case a pair of beds is more suitable. Dimensions and proportions will vary, according to the size of the surrounding garden and the enthusiasm of the gardener. But if the proportions are gen-

In a border at Upton House, a flowering elderberry bush, behind the brick wall on the left, adds height, lifting the eye from ground level.

Opposite: A twin border is separated by a grass path that runs steeply downhill toward the lake at Upton House, adjacent to the kitchen garden. Its character is determined by its slanted site as well as by its vivid flowers. Orange-red poppies offer a striking contrast to the blue campanulas, polemoniums, delphiniums, veronicas, and irises that bloom in early July.

Overleaf: A ten-foot stone wall backs the huge perennial border at Pusey House, Oxfordshire. It is a border of unsurpassed beauty and size. Mr. and Mrs. Michael Hornby's carefully planted color schemes and graduated harmonies are the legacy of Gertrude Jekyll. There are over seventy-five varieties of flowers in this border, among them potentillas, phlox, dahlias, asters, digitalis, salvias, verbascums, nicotianas, agapanthus, antirrhinums, as well as roses, poppies, delphiniums, peonies, and campanulas.

Pusey's perennial border is wide enough to require a side edging consisting of nepetas, poppies, and white campanulas.

Opposite: The tall wrought-iron gate provides a welcome interruption in the long wall and adds a focal point to the border at Pusey House. The border's mixed colors and overall airiness create the appearance of an intensified meadow. A border of this caliber, with its succession of blooms, demands great horticultural skill and almost constant attention. Poppies, meadowrue, campanulas, and roses can be seen at their peak in June.

erous and the planting is lavish, a proper perennial border can convincingly carry an entire garden that is set in otherwise simple surroundings.

Of equal importance is the path that is laid alongside the border. Attention should be given to its tone and texture, for its visual impact should not be underestimated. Broad turf paths or panels of open lawn are particularly flattering, as their green grass offsets the colors and textures of the flowers. If a crisp line between the turf and the border creates an awkward sense of containment a line of brick or stones can be set along the front edge between the turf and the flowers. This will allow plants to billow without the risk of being nipped by a lawnmower. Where heavier foot traffic is likely to pass, a more practical path can be made of firmly packed earth, pieces of stone, or fine gravel, with edges softened by irregular mounds of plants.

To best display a broad variety of flowers, perennial borders are planted in at least three tiers, beginning with the front-of-the-border plants, then gradually building up to the tall background specimens such as delphiniums, hollyhocks, and Eremurus lilies. The number of tiers is determined by the width of the border, and the width, in turn, reflects the size of the garden space, the height of the surrounding walls, and the length of the border itself. The flowers are planted in horizontal drifts rather than in clumps to achieve an interwoven effect. Above all, the groupings must not be rigid.

Low, ground-hugging plants edge the front of the border, easing the transition between the path and the taller masses of flowers. Campanulas, dwarf pinks, and true

A wrought-iron gate that leads to a perennial border, set at the foot of an old brick wall, adds a charming touch to the garden of Rousham House, Oxfordshire.

geraniums form cheerful cushions of color. Plants with handsome leaves that hold their form throughout the growing season, such as hostas, bergenias, irises, alchemillas, and artemisias, are useful, as are low-growing plants that leaf out early.

The heart of the border is the middle strip, where the greatest numbers of plants are concentrated. They should be of medium height, and grouped in companies of three or more, as many perennials are delicate plants that would be lost in a smaller concentration. It is much better to enlarge a successful group of flowers than to repeat it on a small scale. Drifts should vary in size to avoid monotonous rhythms; the larger they are, the more impressive, especially when seen from the side, where foreshortening can reduce even the most substantial-looking clump to a mere speck of color. An occasional achillea brought up to the front line can be added for interest, and is airy enough to allow glimpses through to the flowers behind. Height is an important dimension in the center section, and in the loosest, loveliest schemes it can be achieved by building up in irregular blocks. Sometimes this arrangement is effective in hiding the bare patches left by lupines, Oriental poppies, or similar flowers that have the habit of disappearing early.

Toward the back of the border, plants are used primarily for bulk and silhouette. Tall stands of hollyhocks, alliums, echinops, and plume poppies often alternate with clouds of white-flowering crambe and old-fashioned roses. Spiky plants have strong architectural value, but they can look unnaturally stiff if they are all the same height. Delphiniums, for instance, tend to grow in nicely graduated ranks, while lupines settle in as level blocks of bloom. Pinching back a few front stalks helps to produce a softer line and extends the flowering period.

To produce a sequence of staggered blooms is an arduous task, even with good planning and constant pinching. A perennial border will always be demanding. Some of the plants take several seasons to get established; others require multiple transplantings before they find a permanent place among complementary companions. Most plants have to be lifted and divided every few years, the rampant ones more frequently. Many need staking, a tedious but necessary chore, as the majority of the bigger flowers have a tendency to grow untidily and cannot withstand wind or heavy rain. In other words, a truly glorious perennial border is indeed one of the most labor-intensive garden features.

Two names are virtually synonymous with the perennial border: William Robinson and Gertrude Jekyll. These talented and imaginative nineteenth-century British gardeners were the leading advocates of this style. An irascible and outspoken fellow, William Robinson had an ingrained hatred for Victorian gardening. In particular, he abhorred those flat ornamental bedding schemes in primitive and garish colors, composed of red salvias, orange cannas, yellow calceolarias, blue lobelias, and powder-blue ageratum, that can still be seen in public parks and that sometimes take the form of a clock or spell out the name of a town. Usually, the tender (that is, exotic) plants are nurtured at great expense in greenhouses and set out laboriously into rigid patterns after the last frost. William Robinson is said to have expressed his disgust with

The old city wall serves as a solid backbone to this substantial border at New College, Oxford. Shrubs and small trees planted throughout the border help offset the size of the wall.

tender plants, and terminated his first job as a gardener in Ireland by opening the vents to his employer's greenhouses on a cold winter night. This may only be a legend, but his next position at the Royal Botanic Society's garden in Regent's Park in London was more to his liking; he was to look after the herbaceous gardens. Eventually, he wrote several books advocating the development of an informal style of flower gardening, with loosely arranged and permanent plantings that consisted entirely of hardy species. As he became especially fond of British wild flowers, and advocated their addition, he decided to call his new flower gardens "English." Borders were the most logical place for flowering plants, insisted Robinson: "... there is no arrangement of flowers more graceful, varied, or capable of giving more delight, and none so easily adapted to almost every kind of garden."

Although Robinson did not invent the herbaceous border—the first ones (a pair, at Arley Hall in Cheshire) are said to have originated around 1845—he did liberate his contemporaries from the horticultural limitations of the Victorian brocaded beds. He emphasized plants over pattern and set the stage for the popularization of the perennial border as well as other settings such as dells and woodland gardens. As the founder and publisher of the magazine *The Garden*, he was in a position to shape and educate the public's attitude toward hardy plants and native habitats. His influence has endured more than a century, as we see evidenced by the many contemporary gardens that reflect his horticultural ideas.

His friend and compatriot, Gertrude Jekyll, applied her consid-

*Opposite: The twin border at Westwell Manor, Oxfordshire, is Mrs. Anthea Gibson's contemporary interpretation of Gertrude Jekyll's approach to color. She uses the flowers and leaves of lamb's ears (*Stachys lanata*), erigerons, true geraniums, aconitums, pinks, and campanulas to create a lovely mixture of grays, blues, and greens. With the addition of tall grasses, the border takes on an airy look.*

Above: Crambe cordifolia, *Eremurus lilies, Russell lupines,* Macleaya, *or plume poppies, and a* Rosa rubrifolia *are the tall plants used for the back of a border at Westwell Manor.*

Below: Geraniums, *astrantias, thalictrum, anchusas, erigeron, linaria, salvias, and verbascums mingle their subtle colors in tonal borders at Westwell Manor.*

erable artistic and horticultural abilities to transforming a collection of hardy flowers into a distinctive garden feature. Jekyll was a gifted colorist who, when her eyesight failed, created pictures with masses of plants, using color, form, and texture in the garden just as she did on canvas. First, she built a framework of solid-looking "architectural" plants—evergreens and large-leaved species such as bergenia, acanthus, or yucca; then she filled in with masses of flowers, using warm and cool colors to order the overall composition. Her borders appeared effortless, particularly to those who had associated hardy plants and wild flowers with minimal care; but as Jekyll modestly suggested, the truth lay elsewhere:

> Those who do not know are apt to think that hardy flower gardening of the best kind is easy. It is not easy at all. It has taken me half a lifetime merely to find out what is best worth doing, and a good slice of another half to puzzle out ways of doing it.

This quote appears in her book *Colour Schemes for the Garden*, a title that indicates the significance of color for her.

Color schemes and graduated harmonies were indeed the salient features of her garden at Munstead Wood in Surrey. She not only had an enormous perennial border, 200 feet long by 14 feet wide, but other ones as well, which were done in a narrower spectrum of colors. There was one made entirely of blues, purples, and yellows, as well as her famous Michaelmas daisy border, which bloomed in late summer in hues of pinks and purples. Tonal borders of this kind were

Jekyll's invention and specialty, as were gardens composed of plants blooming in a single color, especially of white flowers in combination with silver foliage plants, and those with glaucous leaves and opalescent color. Miss Jekyll's use of white was unprecedented and has influenced all flower gardening. Endowed with the analytical skill of the professional painter, she formulated her color theories and compared creating a garden or a border to painting a picture with plants; the success of the whole depended on a carefully composed palette. She believed that warm colors are most effectively arranged in harmonies; whereas cool blues and grays are best used in contrasts, offset by pale yellows and pastel pinks. Generally, warm colors are more powerful than cools; a spot of red carries the same visual weight as a mass of blue, for instance. And striking though they may be at close range, strong contrasts look muddy from a distance: blue anchusas next to scarlet poppies appear to be a good match from five feet, but from fifteen feet the combination becomes purplish and dark, creating a hole between brighter patches of color. Subtler contrasts are what make her schemes so convincing. Never before in garden history had color been such an important component, let alone an overriding issue. When the Victorians discovered the brilliance of the primary colors of exotic bedding plants, they indulged in them in a childlike fashion. It took a person like Gertrude Jekyll to develop and encourage the taste for muted color that is now accepted as a sign of sophistication.

The perennial border is the best place for color, whether expressed as a riot of bloom in all shades or

A simple border, at Snowshill Manor, a National Trust property in the Cotswolds, dominated by Oriental poppies and the ubiquitous Alchemilla mollis, leads down to a medieval dovecote.

Overleaf: Much written about but seldom seen are the bizarre delights of Victorian carpet bedding. At Hampton Court, a big border is devoted to a mixture of plants with colorful leaves: coleus, decorative cabbage, ruby chard, and Dusty Miller.

in a single one. Regardless of personal inclinations, nature will provide the predominant palette for each season. Dazzling contrasts are what make the early garden brilliant, with strongly colored tulips and primulas, and later, deep blue irises and salmon poppies. Gradually peonies, lupines, and columbines begin to bloom in paler tones, predicting gentler harmonies ahead. By midsummer the border blooms in sophisticated hues: full-blown drifts of pinks shimmer below delphiniums and campanulas; mounds of true geraniums appear in every shade of pink and bluish purple, enhanced by the soft yellows of Moonshine achilleas and gray-leaved plants. Then in late summer, nature shifts to the yellows, oranges, and purples of asters, dahlias, and chrysanthemums alongside dusky-colored sedums and delicate Japanese anemones. As fall approaches and flowers fade, it is the plants with good leaves and sturdy habits that become more prominent. It is time for the border to go to sleep, before starting its cycle with renewed vigor the following year.

Opposite: Despite New York's hot summer climate, this perennial border of New Dawn roses, irises, feverfew, and delphiniums, at Old Westbury Gardens, Long Island, continues to flourish.

VI

The Italian School

One of the many fountains at the Villa Medici, Rome.

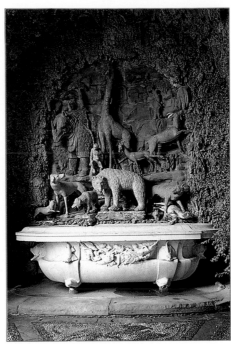

One of the three animal groups found in the grotto of the Villa Medici di Castello, near Florence. It was already an attraction for travelers during the sixteenth century. Water as well as grottoes are key elements in the Italian garden, providing both refreshment and shade from the hot Mediterranean sun.

Preceding page: A shady garden at the Villa Medici, situated on the Pincian Hill in Rome, harbors an ancient sarcophagus and other Roman antiquities. The intrinsic charm of Italian gardens lies in the remarkable blending of nature, architecture, and historical relics.

Opposite: The rustic fountain is a particularly attractive feature in this late sixteenth-century garden at the Villa Aldobrandini, in Frascati, near Rome. In this natural setting, embellished by a grotto, the water source is on the highest point of the property. The channeled water undergoes various stages of design, reaching its final destination, the water theater near the villa, in its most elaborate form.

During the Renaissance, urbane Italians retreated to the countryside to escape from the heat of the Mediterranean summers and the pestilence of the crowded cities. This practice, known as *villeggiatura*, led them to commission the construction of splendid villas high in the hills around Florence and Rome where they could take advantage of cool, cleansing breezes and enjoy views of the plains below.

Virtually all the patrons of these great fifteenth-century country estates were wealthy, well-educated men, for whom nature was a source of tremendous pleasure. Familiar with the architectural traditions of classical antiquity, they favored an ancient building style that blurred the lines between interior and exterior living spaces. Thus, their gardens became integral parts of their villas. No longer considered mere plots for growing and collecting plants, as they had been in medieval times, the gardens of Renaissance Italy came to be conceived as outdoor rooms where civilized activities could be carried on in the open air.

Designers were challenged to build gardens that reflected these contemporary tastes and, at the same time, conformed to the uneven Italian terrain. Initially, their plans were rather haphazard adaptations of the medieval *hortus conclusus*; but as the Renaissance progressed, gardens became increasingly ordered, with symmetrical parts arranged along a central axis. Terraces were chiseled out of hillsides to create separate garden rooms overlooking the Italian landscape. Different levels were bound together by axes and cross-axes in the form of paths, watercourses, colonnaded loggias, vine-draped pergolas, and shaded allées. Grand

Above: At the Villa d'Este, water is displayed in every possible form—springs, cascades, streams, pools, sprays, and water games.

Right: A water display at the Villa d'Este has a most advantageous site—perched on a very steep hill.

Opposite: A niche is revealed at the heart of the massive Fontana dell' Organo (Organ Fountain) at the Villa d'Este, Italy's most famous water garden. The force of the water is used to activate an organ built into the upper part of the fountain.

Above: The Fountain of Diana stands at the foot of a 78-meter-high cascade in the park of the Palazzo Reale in Caserta. A monumental garden, designed in the grand French manner, it contains many Roman and Renaissance elements.

Left: The very long Viale delle Cento Fontane, or Terrace of the Hundred Fountains, in the gardens of the Villa d'Este, is decorated with mossy sculptures of eagles, obelisks, small boats, and heraldic symbols.

The Personification of the Apennines, *a sculpture by Ammanati, rises out of a pool, shivering with cold, in the* bosco, *the wilder part of the gardens at the Villa Medici di Castello.*

*A*bove: *Russell Page designed a neoclassical Italian garden in Moncalieri, near Turin.*

*B*elow: *The use of parterres was an Italian tradition long before it became a French one. Particularly appealing is one executed in box and the more tender* Santolina chameaecyparissus, *or cotton lavender. To create a rich effect, the santolina is sheared an inch higher than the boxwood.*

*O*pposite: *The view here extends the parterre, toward the villa and staircase, an essential element in terraced gardens.*

stone staircases and sweeping ramps were built to mark changes in grade, and elaborate waterworks were employed to channel natural springs. The selection of plants, however, was restrained.

The villa itself sat at the property's highest point, commanding the best view of the garden and the countryside beyond. Surrounding it were the most formal terraces, embellished with low beds lined with precisely clipped herbs and shrubs laid out in simple patterns. They were the primary plants here. With such low planting, the ground immediately around the house was exposed to the full heat of the Mediterranean sun—although that hardly seems appropriate to the *villeggiatura* notion of a shady country retreat. These expansive parterres balanced the building's bulk, however, and such symmetry was considered essential to a properly proportioned scheme.

The farther the garden rooms were from the house, the greener, the shadier, and the more enclosed they were likely to be. It was customary for one of the smaller terraces to be used for dining. This area usually encompassed a wall fountain, a table, and shade trees whose canopy served as a leafy roof. At the Villa Lante, which is a particularly fine example of an early Renaissance garden, the dining terrace includes a stone table with a rivulet channeled through a trough on top. The trough brought water up to diners' fingertips, and was an inviting spot for chilled wine.

The influence of classical Rome is clearly evident in one of the popular features of the Renaissance garden—the outdoor theater. Those on the grandest scale contained a stage circumscribed by terrace walls and adorned with columns and niches occupied by marble heroes

*O*ne of four roof gardens at Rockefeller Center in New York, facing Fifth Avenue.

*P*receding overleaf: The Italian Roof at Rockefeller Center, New York, is a good example of imported style. Interestingly, the building is located on the former site of the Elgin Botanical Gardens. Paul Manship designed the sculptures as well as the famous bronze one of Prometheus at the entrance.

and heroines of classical mythology. Simpler theaters were constructed primarily of plants, with staggered blocks of yew set just far enough apart to allow actors access to and from the wings. Often pieces of sculpture were set in leafy recesses, or embrasures, that were cut out of the enclosing hedges.

Tucked somewhere within the garden would be a *giardino segreto*, an outdoor room that was walled and set below or to the side of the principal terraces. It was segregated, but not necessarily secret, although that is how the term is often translated. For noblemen and papal delegates whose gardens were public spectacles, the *giardino segreto* offered a private place where solitude and serenity were assured. It was also where horticultural and artistic whims could be indulged, such as the planting of a lavish assortment of flowers or herbs or the creation of fanciful topiaries. Within the walls of the *giardino segreto*, the layouts were as varied as the patrons: The Villa Medici's was a simple parterre with clipped box, a central fountain, trees for shade, and several stone benches; the Villa Castello's was a collection of medicinal herbs; and the Villa Farnese's was, and still is, a grassy terrace, with a beautiful view punctuated by dusky spires of cypress and great stone caryatids standing guard in eerie silence.

Parterre, dining room, theater, and *giardino segreto*—each garden room was defined by an enclosing element. Away from the house, hedges of yew, privet, or Grecian bay framed green rooms; in the far reaches of the garden, shady bosks of chestnut, plane, or holm oak defined looser spaces, with their canopies providing protection overhead. Stone walls structured many of the garden rooms, either as free-standing elements or as massive retaining walls buttressing the hillsides. Loggias, pillared pergolas, and open balustrades carried the masonry work into the landscape, extending the lines and proportions of the house out into the most architectural of the outdoor spaces.

Toward the end of the fifteenth century, masons and garden architects acquired a taste for the semicircular forms of curved walls and rounded staircases. Circles and hemispheres were part of the classical architectural vocabulary—most notably as used in ancient coliseums, in the temple at Delphi, and the arcade that surrounded the Canopus at Hadrian's Villa—and Renaissance men appreciated both their historical and design value. To relieve the straight lines of axes and walls, garden makers were liberal in their use of half-rounds and hemispheres; and, thus, their spaces were inviting and extraordinarily gracious.

In addition to defining the outdoor rooms, stonework helped to furnish them, most often in association with water. Cascades were designed to tumble over walls and settle in broad basins beneath the watchful eyes of sculpted Neptunes or gigantic sea serpents. Stone staircases traversed the terraces, and fountains decorated the landings. Some gardens included grottoes—deliciously cool retreats that often marked the source of the garden's water; others featured shady recesses called nymphaeums that were believed to be the favorite haunts of nymphs and good-natured garden spirits.

As a reminder of man's place in nature, sculpted figures were prominently mounted in many Italian gardens. Stony poets and muses, often life-size, offered inspiration, particularly when set near the stage

*O*verleaf: The Canopus at Hadrian's Villa near Tivoli was built by the emperor in memory of his trip to Egypt. Canopus was an ancient city on a tributary of the Nile. Gardens are often built to evoke other places and times.

*F*ollowing overleaf: The garden of the Villa Lante is the jewel of Italian Renaissance gardens. Its plan is determined by a central axis of water, which runs downhill to the four-square fountain in the middle of the lowest terrace.

The terraced garden at the Villa Rufolo in Ravello, near Amalfi, a palazzo dating from the eleventh century with Arab and Norman touches, overlooks the countryside. The garden was last made famous by Richard Wagner, who supposedly received his inspiration there for the motif of Klingsor's magic garden in Parsifal.

Preceding overleaf:
Many people consider Dumbarton Oaks in Washington, D.C., to be the finest and most distinguished garden in the United States. Strongly influenced by the Italian Renaissance style, it consists of a series of terraces, ingeniously fitted together on a hillside. Found throughout are exquisite stonework, steps, staircases, balustrades, urns, finials, gates and garden seats, which have all been individually designed.

Opposite: The garden at the Villa Rufolo combines palm trees with carpet bedding. A high-maintenance garden, it requires the attention of a head gardener and several helpers.

of an outdoor theater; elsewhere various deities, mythological beings, and historical characters graced rooms and walks. Sculpture also served as focal points, thus giving a sense of balance and structure to these outdoor spaces.

Gods and goddesses occupied niches or alternated with columns in porticoes; finials, urns, birds, and fantastic beasts decorated stone balustrades. Where masonry walls gave way to clipped hedges, free-standing statues called terms punctuated the ends of the dark green corridors, terminating garden vistas with a bright and distinctly civilized touch.

Renaissance gardens were not considered completely furnished unless they incorporated water. Since springs dotted the Italian hills, the supply was plentiful, and with the terrain's steep grades, the potential for waterworks was practically limitless. One of the simplest details is used at the Villa Marlia—a single jet rising from a round pool that marks the point where two paths cross. A more elaborate fountain was developed at the Villa d'Este, with a hundred tiny sparkling sprays called lights that spurt from a low moss-covered wall. Water enhances these gardens in the same way that color enriches a well-composed flower garden: without it, the parterres and bosks would be lovely but lifeless. As it runs across terraces, gathering in torrential currents on one level and breaking into delicate rivulets on another, the sound of the water is as rich and cooling as the movement; and both are carefully orchestrated to complement the grand plan.

Water was not used merely as ornament; it also served to emphasize the shifts between levels, to punctuate the points where paths crossed, and to create a natural axis

A sculpture of a female figure graces the circular open-air temple in the bosco *of the Villa Rizzardi in the Valpolicella.*

Garden tools are stored in front of a wall-sized mosaic in a niche below the main terrace of the garden at the Castello Balduino.

Preceding overleaf:
The elaborate baroque terrace, with its topiary yews, at the Castello Balduino in Montalto di Pavia was boldly positioned on a difficult site—a hilltop. Two cypress trees frame the view of the land below.

Opposite: The lowest terrace at the Villa Garzoni in Collodi, a garden dating from about 1650, reflects both Renaissance and baroque influences. One wonders whethers the fantastic yew hedges inspired the writer Carlo Collodi to begin his novel Pinocchio *in the kitchen of the villa.*

as it flowed downhill. At the Villa Lante, for example, water is the primary axis; a stream fed by a natural spring begins at the top of the site and cuts through the center of the garden, becoming increasingly controlled as it progresses downhill. It gurgles over a *cordonate* shaped like a crayfish (a play on the benefactor's name, Cardinal Gambara), then washes over a pair of reclining river gods, is lifted up to channel across a stone table, and finally comes to rest in four still pools at the foot of twin casinos. Plan and planting reinforce the transition from the untamed garden above to the more structured architectural spaces below. The design is remarkably simple, and perhaps for that reason it has weathered the past four hundred years gracefully. In fact, most Italian gardens age relatively well, for their orderly plans, abundant stonework, and uncomplicated planting persist even in the face of prolonged neglect.

In terms of waterworks, the most spectacular Italian garden is the Villa d'Este near Rome, with its tremendous *jet d'eau*, the fountain of a hundred lights, a water organ, and a barrage of conceits designed to drench unwary walkers. Water tricks provided great amusement during the fifteenth century; and even though they are not a common feature in gardens today, a surprise soaking from a hose or sprinkler is still guaranteed to evoke squeals of delight. Such gimmicks are not respectful of rank; they have a frivolous and occasionally licentious aspect as well, which must have undermined both the modesty and decorum of their Renaissance targets, and contributed to their appeal. But not all tricks involved dousing the unsuspecting. One fountain at Aldobrandini, for example, had a jet that could spray

The stage of the green theater at the Villa Marlia, near Lucca, is appropriately decorated with the commedia dell'arte *figures of Arlecchino, Pulcinella, and Colombina. Originally constructed for the Orsetti family in the seventeenth century, the garden is divided into many garden rooms.*

Opposite, above: In 1796, Luigi Trezza designed the green theater at the Villa Rizzardi in the Valpolicella. Its tiers are edged with clipped box, and a promenade on top is enclosed by hedges, niches, and statues. The garden is kept in excellent condition by Count Rizzardi, and the theater is still used for performances.

Opposite, below: Located behind the Villa Aldobrandini is a semicircular nympheum, or water theater. The hedge above the elaborate stone wall acts as an architectural extension of the wall and encloses its famous water staircase. In the niche below is a fountain containing a sculpture of Atlas, the ultimate recipient of the waterfall.

a fine mist, then sparkle in twinkling stars, rain like hailstones, and burst into a dazzling display of liquid fireworks. At the Villa d'Este, the water organ had an equally impressive range, but it concentrated on sound rather than sight—bombarding, chirping, and banging between its presentation of ordinary organ tunes.

Clearly, the pursuit of pleasure was a serious activity for Renaissance craftsmen. Although not all of their handiwork survives, many of the garden rooms that they created are remarkably well preserved. These are slightly worn and somewhat overgrown now, but their bones are intact, and the finely scaled and humanly proportioned spaces within their hedges and walls continue to inspire garden artists and admirers. In recent years, the Italian garden has enjoyed another Renaissance, of sorts—not in the form of an imitative revival, but in terms of adaptive re-use. In the 1950s, landscape architect Thomas Church made outdoor living spaces an indispensable feature of the Californian lifestyle; more recently, many post-modern architects have featured green Italian-inspired rooms in conjunction with their residential plans. The appeal of outdoor garden rooms is not specifically attached to any particular situation or style, however—for twentieth-century designers everywhere are striving to create efficient, livable spaces that combine the best features of indoors and out.

VII

The French Style

A sculpture of a dog sits in the park of Courances. One of the most beautiful classic French gardens, Courances derives its name from the many springs that fill its canals, pools, basins, moats, and cascades with sparkling clear water.

Preceding page: The North Parterre at Versailles, like other French gardens in the grand manner, requires manpower as its vital ingredient. It demands endless hours of maintenance: shearing, clipping, mowing, and raking.

Opposite: The straightness of the poplars lining a canal at Courances is accentuated by a low clipped hedge. All French gardens contain some combination of water, trees, stone, and grass.

Overleaf, left: Still waters surround La Foulerie, a building formerly used for soaking flax in the Parc de Courances.

Overleaf, right: The main axis, as seen from the Château de Courances, leads the eye across an embroidered parterre to a rectangular basin set into the lawn. Its green borders are defined by chestnut trees and sculptures.

The classic French gardens of the seventeenth century were built with arrogance and armies. At Vaux-le-Vicomte, three villages were razed to assure enough space for the proposed chateau and garden, and 18,000 men were employed in the course of construction. At Versailles, sandy marshland was transformed into a garden fit for a king—a Herculean task that required the help of 6,000 horses and more than 22,000 men. Swamps were drained, terraces were created, and waterways were excavated —one called the Pièce d'Eau des Suisses was constructed by the soldiers of the Swiss guard. At Marly, where Louis XIV established a more intimate retreat, the surrounding hills were recontoured; forests of mature trees were planted and then replanted overnight when nearly half of them died; and as the king was especially fond of fountains, an enormous waterworks was assembled, with thirteen waterwheels.

Immense scale and engineered sites best expressed the seventeenth-century Frenchman's desire and ability to control nature. Each garden was based on a precise geometric plan, consisting of terraces, pools, and paths balanced along a central axis. The layouts were monumental—static compositions expressed in rigid forms and inert materials that projected the desired image of endurance and stability. Most of the scheme was visible in a single glance, expressly designed to evoke awe in all who saw it. The view along the primary axis stretched far into the distance, as if to suggest that the patron's control extended infinitely. Within the garden, flat sheets of water, elegantly thin fountains, and topiary trees reinforced the fact that

nature had been tamed by human hands.

The seventeenth century was an age of reason, and its ruling spirit was Descartes, the philosopher and mathematician who introduced the science of analytical geometry. Descartes' configuration of axes and cross-axes applied readily to landscapes, and also reflected court life, wherein the king was the central coordinate around which the entire society revolved. The design of Versailles gives substance to this concept: the *chambre du roi* sits in the center of the chateau and attendants and courtiers were positioned in adjacent rooms, according to their rank. The garden's main axis begins in the king's bedchamber, assuring that the most perfect view be reserved for his royal eyes. The notion that an entire 100-hectare garden (250 acres) could be conceived as emanating from a single point epitomizes Louis XIV's hubris as well as the prevailing French style. Beneath the perfectly controlled geometry was the conviction that nature is beautiful only when ordered by human hands. Men in general, and the seventeenth-century French patrons of art and culture in particular, clearly thought they belonged at the heart of all things considered civilized.

The compulsive application of order and logic permeated other aspects of seventeenth-century life as well, especially in the complicated etiquette attached to the various hierarchies of court society. Days at Versailles and the neighboring chateaux consisted of an elaborately choreographed series of activities that underscored the importance of the monarchy. Louis XIV occupied center stage, and even his most intimate activities, from waking up and dining to playing a round of cards or touring

Louis XIV, in his itinerary for the gardens at Versailles, particularly recommended the view from the Fountain of Apollo, across the tapis vert, *toward the chateau.*

Opposite: The circular pool is situated in one of the more intimate areas at Versailles, the Green Hall near the Trianon.

Overleaf: An allée d'eau *reflects the graceful, free-growing trees (beech, oak, ash, and lime) that make Courances a truly remarkable place. The park is exquisitely maintained by its present owners, the Marquis and Marquise de Ganay.*

*P*ower, control, and
symmetry emanate from the Château de
Vaux-le-Vicomte, André Le Nôtre's first success. The view from the terrace above the
grotto may well have inspired Louis XIV to
throw the chateau's owner, Fouquet, into
prison in 1661 and to initiate plans for designing a garden and palace at Versailles.

A view at the Parc de Sceaux extends across a formal cascade perpendicular to the main axis. The far perspective is typical of Le Nôtre, the designer, who usually allowed for the grandest of views along the main axis and cross-axis as well as for groves and boskets tucked away in the woods.

*The Château de Beloeil
in Belgium is surrounded by an eighteenth-
century park designed in the grand manner of
Le Nôtre. Miles of six-meter-high hornbeam
hedges divide the huge park into green rooms
and corridors.*

the garden, were transformed into public functions. A strict code of manners evolved, dictating such customs as hat raising and curtseying. Forks were introduced at the dining table, and the dance of the century, the minuet, required both rigidity and grace.

Geometry and logic were also responsible for bringing formality to the French garden. Abstract plans were methodically worked out on paper before being imposed upon the landscape. Nature was forced to conform to design: hills were reshaped or removed, to be replaced by flat parterres; water was contained in geometric pools. Trees were set in straight lines; turf was restricted to crisp-edged rectangles. Both trees and shrubs were rendered with such severe pruning that they were left looking more architectural than natural. It was an age devoted to overt expressions of power, and nowhere was this prevailing spirit more apparent than in the garden. Obvious and pronounced artistry was the fashion: the more elaborate the design and elegant its embellishments, the more prestige it conferred upon its patron.

The man who translated seventeenth-century power and politics into parterres was Andre Le Nôtre, a trained gardener, or *jardiniste*, whose humility and exquisite taste tempered the excesses of the Sun King's court. Le Nôtre was born to a gardening family: his father had been the royal gardener at the Tuileries (a post that his son inherited), his grandfather was a gardener, and both of his sisters had married gardeners. He was a modest man—the coat of arms he designed for himself bore a spade surrounded by slugs and topped with cabbage leaves. Like all well-educated seventeenth-century

Frenchmen, Le Nôtre had toured Italy and was a student of the arts. Most important, he had a keen ability to perceive the needs of his royal patrons: he understood that massive scale, seemingly infinite vistas, and awe-inspiring plans were what the times required.

Le Nôtre's true genius lay in his restraint. Rather than indulge in flamboyancy, as often happens when power and wealth merge, he developed an elegant, refined style —an achievement that is all the more impressive in light of the extremely exaggerated scale at which he worked. Vaux-le-Vicomte, his first significant commission as a landscape designer, proved a splendid beginning: the chateau rises up out of a surrounding moat, commanding a sweeping view of parterres patterned with turf, red gravel, low evergreen hedges, and elegantly detailed pools. The plan is open and ordered—a unified composition balanced along a broad central path. The parterres descend very gradually, separated by a series of shallow steps that are barely visible from above. Masonry is kept to a minimum, as Le Nôtre preferred to use plants to structure and embellish his gardens. Cones of yew serve as a sculptural counterpoint to the extremely flat parterres; banks of sheared trees line the edges of the garden. In the surrounding boskets, Le Nôtre cleared small outdoor rooms that provided welcome relief from the heat, glare, and vast expanse of the parterres.

Vaux-le-Vicomte was built for Nicolas Fouquet, Louis XIV's Finance Minister—a wealthy man devoted to the arts, whose taste proved to be better than his judgment. When the twenty-three-year-old king first saw the chateau, its extravagance sent him into a jealous rage. Within three weeks,

Above: Within the ornamental parterre at the Château de Villandry are the symbolic jardins d'amour. *The "broken hearts" of passionate love were executed in boxwood and filled with seasonal flowers.*

Below: Set below an allée of lime trees and a classical staircase is the Maltese Cross parterre at the Château de Villandry.

*T*opiary has been boldly executed upon this yew at the Château de Rambouillet to achieve the shape of a pointed cube.

*O*pposite: The French used boxwood exclusively for their parterres. Evergreen, the shrub has many advantageous features: it can be cut into any shape, it grows very slowly, and it will live for years. Beyond the detailed parterre de broderie at Vaux-le-Vicomte is an arcaded grotto and a slope on which a statue of Hercules stands.

*O*verleaf: An allée of cone-shaped yews makes an attractive feature at the Parc de Sceaux. After the death of Louis XIV, the park fell into decay and was not reconstructed until the late 1930s. According to Russell Page, reconstructions are usually influenced by the style that is popular when the restoration takes place.

Louis had issued orders for Fouquet's arrest, arguing that his minister must have dipped into royal coffers to pay for so flamboyant a residence. Fouquet's life was uneventful from then on, as he spent most of it in prison; but his garden set the standard for French style. As soon as the king saw Vaux-le-Vicomte, he knew what he wanted —a setting even more magnificent. He invited Le Nôtre to help him build a garden around a small chateau that had been his father's old hunting lodge at Versailles.

Thus, from the moment of its inception, the garden at Versailles was an expression of Louis XIV's megalomaniacal appetite. The king took a passionate interest in its development. The chateau was to be the stage upon which he played out his life, and he wanted to be actively involved in its creation. He oversaw the constant changes and additions that were carried out during the next fifty years. Urns, vases, and figures had to be cast in plaster first for his approval before being made in marble; he insisted upon three revisions to one of the main parterres. Once construction was complete, Louis XIV wrote a guide with explicit instructions about how to proceed through the garden, dictating precisely where to go and in which direction to look en route.

The garden at Versailles, which was started seven years before the palace, is organized around a central axis that extends as far as the eye can see. To exaggerate the impression of the king's infinite control, the axis was not punctuated at the horizon, except during a short period each year when the setting sun became a brilliant terminus. The scale at Versailles is immense: the main axis marked by the Grand Canal is more than a

mile long. One of the embellishments tucked into the woods is the Grand Trianon, a separate palace set among bright flower gardens, where Louis XIV could escape with his favorite companions and courtesans.

As Louis XIV and Le Nôtre were well aware, monumentality begins with impressive scale, and that, in turn, is a function of vast open space. Thus, the gardens at Versailles were developed as a series of flat, open terraces called parterres—a word adapted from the phrase *broderie par terre*, or embroidery on the ground. The best French parterres were like exquisite needlework, with boxwood stitching highlighted in earthen beds. Crushed stone or brick dust added color, as did flowers which were set out in pots throughout the garden. A main view corridor, or axis, connected the different parterres, stretching between banks of densely planted trees. Allées crisscrossed through the boskets, or woods, beyond, and they were punctuated by *ronds points*—clearings that were used when the women of the court carried picnics into the woods where they could admire their gentlemen riding through. By the seventeenth century, *ronds points* had been adapted to house the grottoes, theaters, aviaries, and water tricks devised by the fifteenth-century Italians. Such frivolities were considered indispensable to a French garden; and tucked into the boskets, they provided a pleasant change of scale and scene without diluting the formal design. The boskets were particularly appealing because they offered an intriguing escape from the main garden, promising privacy, surprise, and intimacy in an otherwise open landscape.

Plants were treated as part of

*E*xuberant fountains
are a delightful feature of Vaux-le-Vicomte.

*O*pposite: Sculptures
have always been favored by the French, who have used them to embellish their gardens. Jean Baptiste Carpeaux's centerpiece for a fountain in the Jardin du Luxembourg depicts the four continents holding up a celestial sphere. It was unveiled in 1874.

*L*ocated in the gardens of the Grand Trianon is this parterre seen between clipped chestnut trees. During Louis XIV's reign, 150,000 flowerpots were set out in the two main parterres. These were changed frequently, as the Sun King enjoyed deus ex machina *effects*.

the architecture in French gardens, for only as consistent, steadfast elements did they enhance the themes of monumentality and control. Few species were spared the gardener's shears: horsechestnuts, hornbeams, lindens, plane trees, acacias, even maples and oaks were given geometric shapes and aligned like soldiers to enclose and enrich garden spaces. Along the central axis, trees were sheared to as high as the highest ladder would reach and left to grow freely above that—a technique called pruning *en rivière* that enforced the architectural illusion by creating a leafy cornice line. Elsewhere, crowns were shaped into cubes or spheres that sat lollipop-like on top of straight stems, or branches were pollarded, creating gnarled fists that sprouted tufts of greenery. Poplars conformed to contemporary tastes without any pruning, and so were a favorite choice for planting along canals.

On the ground, the panels of grass that stretched taut across the terraces were so immaculately preened that they were called *tapis verts*, or green carpets. Gravel paths surrounded the turf and often their edges were marked by low evergreen hedges or clipped cones of boxwood or yew. Sculpture lined the edges of the woods or alternated with topiary along the border between the grass and the gravel. Urns sat on top of pedestals; vases hosted exotic flowering plants; and gods, goddesses, and mythological characters immortalized in marble lent a classic air.

Water, in the form of pools highlighted by frothing fountains or single-plumed *jet d'eau*, was one of the garden's most pleasant ornaments, relieving the extensive open spaces with cool, melodious movement. The flat terrain of France

*L*e Nôtre landscaped
the park of St. Cloud. It was the residence of
Monsieur, Louis XIV's brother, who excelled
at entertaining. Later, it became Napoleon
III's favorite place for holding official recep-
tions. Nineteenth-century gardeners were as
fond of carpet bedding as Louis XIV had
been of flower parterres. On the left side is a
typical Le Nôtre vista. On the right is an
unusual piece of carpet bedding, a ribbon
consisting of ageratum, box, and begonias
planted on a slanting hillside.

Above: At the Château de Maintenon, the Sun King's initial has been cut into the tapis vert. *The garden was designed by Le Nôtre.*

Left: The stunning walls of the Palais du Sport Bercy in Paris are covered with green lawn—a contemporary version of the tapis vert.

Opposite: Four urns define the corners of a classical tapis vert *at St. Cloud.*

Overleaf: The park of the Château de Chantilly is said to have been Le Nôtre's favorite creation. It is unusual because the main axis of the T-shaped plan does not start from the chateau but from the statue of the Grand Condé at the top of the staircase to the left of the building. The mirrorlike sheets of water surrounding the chateau create a softer effect than does the rigidly symmetric layout of other Le Nôtre designs.

was not conducive to elaborate waterworks, but the king and the members of his court loved water and were willing to go to extraordinary lengths and expense to create fountains befitting the scale of their immense terraces. Only major earthworks could assure a plentiful supply of water at Versailles, for instance, but because the king's appetite for fountains was insatiable, the garden is filled with fountains, even though the water supply and pressure were insufficient. Not all of the fountains are operable at once, but their plentiful numbers and the sheer size of the garden help to offset that disadvantage. As the king progressed from fountain to fountain, flags and fleet-footed boys flashed through the surrounding boskets, advising which waters should be extinguished and which turned on in time for the next royal viewing. The system was satisfactory, apparently—Louis XIV thought of Versailles as a water garden, and he referred to touring the garden as seeing the fountains.

People were the true ornaments of the French garden. They introduced color and animation to landscapes that were formidably austere when empty. The gardens themselves were designed as backdrops; the members of the royal court were the actors, and the constant display of pomp and circumstances provided the movement. In addition to the courtiers, endless festivities helped to enliven the gardens: plays were staged in shady outdoor theaters; miniature ships waged war in the canals; music and masterful displays of fireworks filled summer evenings.

Formal gardens are the ultimate place for show, and that may explain why, even in the absence of kings, the French style has re-

The many allées along the streets and boulevards in Paris are clearly the work of man and not nature.

Preceding overleaf: Situated alongside the mile-long Grand Canal at Versailles is this lime tree allée. During the reign of Louis XIV, the allées of plane trees, beeches, horse chestnuts, lime trees (linden), and sometimes oaks were established throughout France on both private and public grounds. These are maintained and renewed with admirable care and concern for future generations.

Opposite: The plane trees alongside a canal leading up to the Château de Courances have been allowed to grow naturally. This is a remarkable feat, since they were planted in 1782, a time when gardeners thought nothing should be left unclipped.

Overleaf: Louis XV, a man with a penchant for privacy, ushered in an age of greater intimacy. In 1750, he added the French Pavilion to the park of the Trianon so that he could rest on his way to the botanical gardens and the menagerie he had erected nearby.

mained a classic means of flaunting power and taste. Victorian gentlemen followed the French fashion by building extensive hothouses to fill their flowery parterres with a dazzling array of exotics and brilliantly colored tender annuals. The larger the beds and the more often they were changed, the greater the impact they had—a tradition that survives today in parks and municipal plantings, where masses of bright flowers sing the proud praise of their local sponsors.

The French style can also be adapted to suit more intimate spaces. Russell Page's garden at the Frick Museum in New York is distinctly French in flavor, with its panel of turf, neat gravel paths, low-lying pool, and pots full of flowers. But to keep the composition from being instantly comprehensible —and therefore dull—Mr. Page varied the scheme. Each of the four central trees is a different species, and their individual placement breaks the rigid four-square geometry of the small space. Both the pool and its single jet are off-center. The elegance essential to French style is retained, but the designer managed to avoid its characteristic uniformity. His irregular touches instilled a certain dynamism that was foreign to the grand French gardens; but in smaller gardens that energy is vital.

Other contemporary interpretations of the classic French style have been carried out by corporations such as PepsiCo in Purchase, New York, and Hershey Chocolate Company in Hershey, Pennsylvania. They have revived Le Nôtre's spirit as they commission garden designers to create parklike grounds for the enjoyment of their employees and the interested public.

VIII

The "English" Garden

Clockwise from upper left: Four different compartments at Hidcote Manor, a National Trust property in Gloucestershire. The White Garden. A view through the Swimming Pool Garden. The Stilt Garden is distinguished by its clipped hornbeams. The gracefully pleached lime allée.

Preceding page: During the beginning of the twentieth century, the English garden evolved as a series of small compartments designed for celebrating the changing seasons with different displays of plants and blossoms. First to bloom in this Sussex garden is a forsythia hedge.

At first glance, an English garden appears to be informal, with its abundance of flowers and looseness of planting. Upon closer inspection, however, it is revealed to be structured tightly around a framework of walls, hedges, beds, borders, and paved pathways. These are the garden's bones, and whether built of stone or made of plants, they create its scale, order, and coherence. If the flowers and shrubs bloom profusely and if the planting is particularly choice, the result will be a truly English garden —formally planned but informally planted.

The woman most often associated with this style was Gertrude Jekyll, an accomplished Edwardian woman: she was well-read, she had traveled widely in her youth, and she exchanged opinions with some of the leading artists and intellectuals of her day. In addition, she painted and was skilled in needlework, silversmithing, and in the emerging art of photography. Today she is best remembered as a writer and an outstanding plantswoman. At the age of fifty, she devoted herself almost exclusively to the fine art of gardening. Her legacy is threefold: she wrote more than a dozen books describing her methods of gardening; she designed more than 200 gardens; and as a gifted writer and able interpreter, she captured and formulated the gardening trends of her time. Expounding the virtues of local custom and indigenous craftsmanship, she was strongly influenced and inspired by the aesthetics of the cottage garden, that is, its uninhibited planting arrangement, its profusion, and its hardy native plants. At the same time, she fully understood the necessity of a firm architectural plan as the underlying structure for a good garden. Her

gardens incorporated such formal features as the main axis, the long view, the *giardino segreto*, and the parterre of the Italian, French, Tudor, and Dutch gardens to suit contemporary taste. Most noteworthy was her adaptation of the sixteenth- and seventeeth-century idea of separate garden compartments, with each garden room given a different treatment.

Miss Jekyll was, of course, not a solitary genius. She collaborated with two equally influential people: first, with William Robinson, the outspoken champion of English wild flowers and hardy species informally grown, and with Sir Edwin Lutyens, a prominent architect. Her adherence to formal plans was in some measure due to her partnership with Lutyens, an extraordinarily versatile designer, comfortable in virtually any style, and like her, passionately interested in native material, craftsmanship, and the vernacular of the Surrey countryside. Miss Jekyll was nearly sixty when they met, he was only twenty-six. The elderly lady and the aspiring architect became loyal friends and ultimately collaborated on over a hundred gardens, creating a unique garden style.

Lutyens designed complicated systems of terraces, walls, steps, sunken pools, parterres, rills, tanks, niches, and pergolas. These were executed in local materials with exquisite detail work, which provided the perfect foil for Jekyll's planting; she sent roses and jasmine rambling over his pergolas, trained clematis and shrubs to cloak the walls, tucked rock plants into the crevices between the stones, and softened the masonry's hard lines with every sort of plant that had the ability to blur edges.

Hestercombe in Cheddon Fitzpaine, Somerset, is a good exam-

A topiary entrance leads *from the round swimming pool to a green annex used as a dressing room.*

*P*receding overleaf: *Boxwood and yew hedges enclose Hidcote's white garden, while plump, Dutch-style topiary doves mark the four corners of the path's intersection. Within are masses of silver-leaved plants and pale flowers.*

*O*pposite: *A sheared copper beech hedge set against the chartreuse green blossoms of* Alchemilla mollis *and the blue-green of the garden benches creates one of the many unusual color schemes at Hidcote.*

*O*verleaf: *A border on the central garden walk at Hidcote Manor is filled with the soft-colored summer and autumn flowers that Gertrude Jekyll favored. The cedar of Lebanon on the right is almost the only garden feature that Major Lawrence Johnston found when he started his garden in 1905 on this windswept hill in the Cotswolds.*

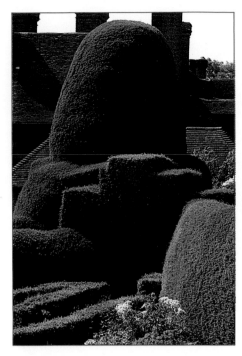

Above and opposite:
The English use topiary to provide an element of fantasy in their gardens, while the French and Italians prefer masonry and sculpture to achieve the same effect. Great Dixter in Sussex has bold, humorous topiaries, designed by Nathaniel Lloyd. Their giant size matches the scale of the house, as does the grand border (upper right) of perennials and shrubs.

ple of the Jekyll-Lutyens collaboration. The garden begins on high ground, adjacent to the house, with a terrace that provides a clear view of the sunken garden below. Long raised walkways line the sides of the plat, or sunken parterre. A stone pergola at the south end encloses the garden, offering glimpses of the Taunton Vale beyond. At the foot of the upper terrace, a gray border creates a pale foreground for misty stands of lavender and nepeta alongside a mixture of flowers of the palest pinks and yellows and many gray-leaved plants. Pastels modulated with grays and glaucous blue-greens are typical of Jekyll's color schemes, as is the combination of cloudy and spiky plant forms. On the east and west sides are two elaborate raised walkways, tailor-made for the herbaceous borders for which she was famous. Each has a central canal, or "rill," set flush in the grass and edged with flagstone that loops around circular tanks, which Miss Jekyll planted with irises, arum lilies, and other water-loving plants. The plat itself is divided diagonally; Lutyens set the stage for horticultural luxuriance by edging the angled bed with a band of stone over which plants can tumble. Throughout the garden, plants soften the masonry lines. Self-seeding valerian and snow-in-summer colonize crevices between steps, and cushions of Erigeron daisies burst out of cracks in the stone walls.

The garden at Hestercombe was restored in the 1970s by the Somerset Fire Brigade, according to a copy of Miss Jekyll's original plan found pinned inside of the potting shed. Today, it stands as one of the few existing examples of the Jekyll-Lutyens partnership.

The basic garden plan that evolved under the influence of Jek-

yll and Lutyens divided the garden into a series of compartments. Near the house, the garden begins as small, formal, or semi-formal outdoor rooms. But order and architecture fade farther away from the house, as the garden scenery becomes progressively greener and wilder, and may incorporate meadows, orchards, and well-tended woodlands, in addition to streams and bogs. The transition to the English countryside is subtle, for the landscape beyond the garden gate is a cultivated domain, with farmers' tidy fields outlined by hedgerows and streams that are marked by the crooked lines of pollarded willows.

Walls and hedges serve as the backbone of the English garden: they outline the spaces and protect the plants, and provide a consistent backdrop for the ever-changing displays of buds and blossoms. Hidcote Manor in Gloucestershire is unparalleled in its extraordinary hedges. Major Lawrence Johnston, the enigmatic American bachelor who spent more than forty years designing and planting its garden, was born in France. While living there, he developed an interest in topiary hedges and pleached allées, which he later incorporated into Hidcote's axial plan. The hedges were necessary to shelter Johnston's prized plants, since the garden is situated high on a windswept hill in the northern Cotswolds.

Hidcote's plan is based on a T-shaped axis. Numerous compartments for flowers are tucked around and between the two perpendicular axes, one of which is called the Long Walk. This runs gradually downhill between blocks of clipped hornbeams. Each of the separate garden compartments is enclosed by hedges of holly, boxwood, yew, or copper beech, and sometimes

Circular steps were one of Edwin Lutyens's favorite architectural details. Snow-in-summer, or Cerastium tomentosum, inhabits the cracks between the steps leading down from the rotunda.

Opposite: A rose climber softens the masonry window in a wall at Hestercombe.

An unusual pleached lime alleé can be found at Alderley Grange in Gloucestershire.

Opposite: A naturally growing Pyrus salicifolia "Pendula," *or weeping-willow-leafed pear tree, thrives at Alderley Grange.*

even by tapestry hedges composed of different plants, with the occasional addition of a climbing *Tropaeolum speciosum*, or flameflower. The Pillar Garden owes its name to an enclosure of twenty-two towering English yews; the Stilt Garden is composed of a double allé of hornbeams with thick, straight trunks and geometrically trimmed tops; an avenue of pleached lime trees makes an archway of cool shade in summer. Perhaps the most remarkable aspect of Major Johnston's hedges is that their main purpose is to surround a staggering collection of plants, grouped in a number of outdoor rooms that boast different themes.

Similar to Hidcote in its basic anatomy, its massive yew hedges, and its dramatic topiary is Great Dixter in Sussex. It, too, is split up into a system of enclosed, separate gardens. Both the restoration of the fifteenth-century manor house and the layout of the garden at Great Dixter were planned by Sir Edwin Lutyens for Nathaniel Lloyd, an architectural historian, topiary enthusiast, and author, whose book on sculpting figures from yew and boxwood is a garden classic. Lutyens introduced such features as a sunken garden, a pergola, a rose garden, and a courtyard garden, while Lloyd was responsible for the unconventional topiary and the hedges that surround the series of gardens arranged in a circuit around the house. (The garden has stayed in the same family and is now tended by Christopher Lloyd, Nathaniel's son, who is an equally accomplished horticulturist.)

The key to the image of profusion and luxuriance that is the quintessence of the English garden is the extraordinary variety of its plants—the flowering shrubs, the

herbaceous perennials, the herbs, the annuals, the bulbs, the wild flowers, and the ground covers. In the Middle Ages, the range of plants in Europe was fairly limited. But with the discovery of the New World many foreign species found their way across the Atlantic to the old country. Botanists, adventurers, and professional plant hunters were sent out on exploratory trips to Africa, South America, and other distant lands to ship home horticultural treasures. For years, however, only captains of merchant ships and missionaries returning from China and Japan were able to import occasional Oriental plants. But when these two countries finally opened their gates to the West, plant exports surged. England was an eager recipient of that bounty and, because of its temperate climate, proved a particularly hospitable ground for a huge number of the foreign species. Italy, on the other hand, never showed much interest in imported plants, and France accepted only the botanical newcomers that would meet specific horticultural requirements and were reliable as to shape and color. The United States, though, was the beneficiary of more than 1,000 species that E.H. "Chinese" Wilson shipped to the Arnold Arboretum in Boston.

The two geniuses capable of selecting and coordinating the mass of plants that were available by the end of the nineteenth century were William Robinson and Gertrude Jekyll. Robinson saw the garden as a place in which rare plants should be displayed. His lightness of touch and genuine botanical respect for plants, their structure, and their habitat helped to change people's sensitivity toward gardening. And Gertrude Jekyll, his colleague, added her taste for color and

Cottage gardeners were among the first to decorate a door with climbing and potted plants. At Barnsley House, a ceanothus mingles its branches with honeysuckle and a variegated shrub.

Nellie Moser clematis, abutilon, and Danse du Feu rambler roses conceal a trellis near a door at Barnsley House, Gloucestershire.

Opposite: In June Rosemary Verey's laburnum walk is in full bloom. The yellow blossoms above are complemented by the Allium flatunense, hostas, and golden lemon balm below.

Overleaf: People from everywhere in the British Isles flock to Sissinghurst to admire Vita Sackville-West's horticultural achievements. She wrote many articles about her plants for The Observer, thus inspiring and educating the public. White wisteria, more desirable than the common blue one, hangs over the wall. In the background, a border of Exbury azaleas is in full bloom; this deciduous type flowers somewhat later than its pink cousins.

Following overleaf: Successful plant association is a goal to which all sophisticated English gardeners aspire. What appears to the novice as one plant is actually a combination of blue-leaved hosta and ornamental onion flowers, which bloom in June. By the time the hosta produces its own blooms in August, the onion flowers will have died and been cut off.

*In the flower world,
the color red offers the greatest variety of
shades from which to choose. There are many
flowers that may be used with roses, or used
separately—such as rose campion,* Geranium
subcaulescens, *and candelabra primulas.*

*Opposite: Flower gar-
dening entails a great deal of work, including
weeding and cutting off flower heads once they
are past their prime to ensure strong, healthy,
and long-blooming plants. The successful
plantings at Sissinghurst are the result of
intensive gardening.*

form as well as her understanding for the need to have a well-structured framework within a natural garden. She said of the design problem:

> The possession of quantity of plants, however good the plants themselves may be and however ample their number, does not make a garden; it only makes a collection. Having got the plants, the great thing is to use them with careful selection and definite intention.

Many people consider Vita Sackville-West the greatest plantswoman of this century. Her approach was painterly, her enthusiasm obvious; as a result, her garden at Sissinghurst is unrivaled in the richness of its planting. Like Hidcote, it is composed of a series of garden rooms; the architectural plans were drawn up by Miss Sackville-West and her husband, Sir Harold Nicholson. She concentrated her attention and her considerable knowledge on the detailed plantings, or "furnishings," that gave each room its distinctive theme. Her White Garden at Sissinghurst is probably the best known. Here, all the flowers are white or gray. Blocks of airy-looking crambe, variegated phlox, nicotiana, antirrhinum, *Dictamnus alba*, and artemisia are planted in bold masses framed by dark green borders of boxwood. Iceberg roses are underplanted with white pulmonarias, and a silver willow-leaved pear tree shades a statue of a virgin with its shimmering foliage. In July, a late-blooming *Rosa longicuspis*, rambling over a delicate iron pergola, highlights the center. The wealth of plants in this small plot alone is overwhelming. "The one

thing I feel sure of," wrote Miss Sackville-West in one of her articles as correspondent for *The Observer*:

is that every odd corner should be packed with something permanent, something of interest and beauty, something tucking itself into something else in the natural way of plants when they sow themselves and combine as we never could combine them with all of our skill and knowledge.

There are many other garden "rooms" at Sissinghurst, all based on a theme and artistic in their design. Maximum attention is given to color and to inspired plant associations. Gay areas of color alternate with quiet interludes of green; near the rose garden, which is largely furnished with old-fashioned roses, is the rondel, a circular patch of lawn enclosed by yew hedges. In addition, there is an orchard filled with apple trees, a moat, and a lime-walk, or spring garden, edged by a border of Exbury azaleas and hostas, a cottage garden, an herb garden, and numerous borders.

Home to Rosemary Verey, another English writer and gardener, is Barnsley House in Gloucestershire. In her garden, a more recent example of the English style, Mrs. Verey combines many of the traditional elements within the relatively small space of a few acres. Among the plantings that recall the past are a pair of Elizabethan knot gardens, a stone path invaded by helianthemums and lined by Irish yews, a pleached lime alley, a tiny, all-green landscape area, and a neoclassical summerhouse that overlooks a pool filled with irises and flanked by an iron gate boldly painted blue. Although there are

The jewel of Sissinghurst is its white garden, probably the most beautiful garden in England. It was not completed until 1950, although Vita Sackville-West made plans for it after World War I. An extraordinary selection of plants having white flowers or silver foliage is grown in profusion within a framework of box-edged beds. An iron trellis in the center is covered by a Rosa longicuspis, *which flowers in July.*

Opposite: Sizable clumps of hosta, polygonatum, Stachys lanata, and other plants build up toward the Crambe cordifolia *and the willow-leaved pear tree on the left. In the garden, behind the tree, is the priest's house, with its facade smothered by roses.*

*T*intinhull House, a National Trust property in Somerset, has a garden that combines formal stonework with informal planting. Paths and hedges divide the garden, which was laid out in the 1930s, into sections. The view is over the circular lily pond at the Queen Anne facade of the house.

*O*pposite: Across the same lily pond is a path, edged by Nepeta fassenii, *or catmint, which leads into the countryside. Irises, foxgloves, artemisias, roses, and pinks add lovely color to the pond area.*

*O*verleaf: The sunken garden at Lyegrove, the site of a former kitchen garden, became an enchanting lily pond under the guidance of the Dowager Countess of Westmorland. It is the epitome of English gardening, as flowers are allowed to grow casually between the cracks of the pavement. Valerians, irises, foxgloves, veronicas, pinks, and rockroses are at their peak in June, just as the water lilies begin to bloom.

*T*he countryside hedge
*of long ago has developed into the garden
fence and hedge of today.*

*D*ry stone walls are
the favorite habitats of rock plants such as
Campanula porten schlagiana, *which flour-
ishes at Hestercombe. Showy white delphiniums adorn the terrace above the wall.*

also several truly outstanding herbaceous borders, the glory of the
garden may well be Mrs. Verey's
laburnum walk and her kitchen
garden, which is fashioned after the
decorative principles of the Château de Villandry, stocked with rose
trees and cabbages. All these parts
are loosely but successfully connected to each other, lending the
garden that casual touch that epitomizes English style and graceful-
ness. Barnsley House includes the
many features and the abundance
of plants that are characteristic of
the English style, but, in adherence to contemporary tastes, the
overall plan is organic. It is structured without being symmetrical;
it has axes and yet is not dominated by straight lines. The garden is a variation upon the theme
of the classic English garden.

*P*receding overleaf:
*What is now a sunken garden on this old
English property in Suffolk was formerly a
farmyard covered in brambles and nettles. It
was converted into a water garden in 1945,
but the roof of the former cattleshed on the
right was retained for use as a pool house.
Rambling on the back wall is an Albertine
rose. Big-leaved, moisture-loving plants such
as bergenias, hostas, and umbrella plants
(*Peltiphyllum peltatum*) flourish at the
water's edge.*

Above: Climbers and profusely flowering perennials and shrubs help to cloak this wall in the Oxford Botanic Garden. A border of tree peonies occupies the right-hand side.

Overleaf: The round wall in Switzerland is made of building elements shaped like fish scales. The space between each scale contains pockets of earth populated by lobelias and geraniums.

Following overleaf: One of the two famous walls of animals and arches encloses the green carpets in the court-yard of the Château de Raray. The wall as a partition is an ingredient typical of the English garden.

IX

The Designed Landscape

Russell Page's garden in Long Island is designed around an elliptical pool. In its initial phases, the landscape movement contained architectural ornaments from other cultures, but new effects were achieved by mixing non-indigenous plants, such as kurume azaleas and evergreens, with the native dogwoods and wild flowers. The exoticism of such a garden, though not the beauty, is obvious only to people with some horticultural knowledge.

Preceding page: It is well worth having a landscape designed around Acer saccharum, *the North American sugar maple. In fall, throughout upstate New York and New England, its leaves present a magnificent show as they turn red, gold, and brown.*

Opposite: A seemingly natural path cuts through the woods on the banks parallel to the elliptical pond. The shrubs are richly underplanted with wood hyacinths, lilies of the valley, and wild strawberries.

Overleaf: The enchanted garden of Ninfa in Sermoneta, Italy, belongs to the Caetani family. It is essentially a jardin anglais *designed around the towers and ruins of an Italian medieval town. Big-leaved* Gunnera manicata *and rose shrubs have been planted along a natural stream in the English style; in other parts, cypress trees and lavender walks remind one of its Mediterranean location.*

The unique combination of sun and soil, trees and terrain that gives each piece of land its special character also serves as the starting point for a landscape garden. The design develops in response to the site and in deference to nature's principles. Trees and shrubs stand grouped in loose masses around open lawns, water gathers in low-lying ponds and streams, a tranquil woodland promises shade—a scene such as this appears to be the work of nature. But, in fact, in a designed landscape this setting represents man's attempt to strike a balance between design and nature. One who achieved that with great mastery is Russell Page, the well-known Englishman who worked in many places, from Italian hillsides to Mediterranean islands, from French and English country gardens to New York city plots. Before he began his design, he looked for a source of inspiration, which he generally found somewhere on the site. But once Page established the principal idea or theme, he did not hesitate to weave his own order into the fabric of the existing landscape. The versatility and elegance with which he used trees and water, in particular, brought him international acclaim. Two woodland gardens, one in northern Italy, the other in the United States, provide excellent examples of the varied ways in which he has employed these two elements to achieve different effects.

In Villar Peroso, on the grounds of Mr. and Mrs. Gianni Agnelli's summer residence at the foot of the Italian Alps in Piedmont, Page managed to build a serene water garden in what was originally a steep and narrow valley, with a torrential stream rushing through in

springtime. Given the sharp grade of the land, the water flowed too quickly to be appreciated as a landscape amenity. To slow it down and provide comfortable niches for plants, Page dammed the stream in eleven places, creating a string of eleven ponds from twenty to fifty feet in diameter, connected by eleven cascades varying from three to nine feet in height. Each pond is surrounded by groups of water-loving plants and shrubs such as kousa dogwoods, *Rhus cotinus*, *Viburnum plicatum mariesii*, and *Hydrangea quercifolia*, underneath or near which scillas, daffodils, and Himalayan poppies make their seasonal appearance. The result is a water garden which, despite the clearing of trees and the removal of earth, looks almost natural.

In a garden in Long Island, Page opted for a solution that is more obviously designed. The plan is restrained, symmetrical, and self-contained. An elliptical pool lies flush in an oval grass glade, the long axis of which is subtly emphasized by a path leading to and from the pool. Azaleas, rhododendrons, dogwoods, and other larger trees are massed on three-tiered rising banks that provide the outer framework of this garden, forming three colorful parallel bands that repeat the oval shape of the pool. The underplanting, which can be seen mainly from two oval paths that divide the bank into upper and lower levels, consists of a rich mixture of woodland hyacinths, lilies of the valley, ferns, mayapples, strawberries, hostas, and rhubarb plants. This treatment and the incorporation of the surrounding landscape produce a surprising informality, despite the garden's prevailing symmetry. In both of these gardens, human interference is felt rather than seen—the total effect is quite natural.

Common to almost every landscape garden are the paths and stretches of open lawn that invite views and exploration. These are the organizing elements, for they connect the various sections of the garden. Perhaps more important, paths direct passage and therefore determine how people perceive the landscape. They serve as informal axes, and the series of openings and enclosures that they pass through are as ordered as the rooms and walls of more formal plans, except that in a landscape garden the elements are arranged loosely, with sweeping lines and curvilinear patterns that are meant to appear natural. Mixed clusters of trees and shrubs are used to create enclosures around irregularly shaped open spaces. Each space, in turn, is planned around a specific feature —perhaps a special tree, a lake, a glimpse of scenery ahead, or a panoramic view.

Movement is fundamental to the perception of the designed landscape, whether it involves walking or letting one's eyes wander. A path disappearing around a bend or a view obscured by branches invites curiosity and anticipation. Thus a sense of mystery or an element of surprise is appropriate to the landscape style. Formal gardens with their strict geometric plans can be viewed in one glance, while informally designed landscapes by definition are ordered asymmetrically and are, therefore, more complex visually. Although the Chinese and the Japanese have employed asymmetric garden design for centuries, Western eyes and minds have been trained to expect symmetry. And when it is not immediately apparent, they seek to establish it, as if to satisfy a need for balance. Asymmetric designs are harder to

An Enkianthus campanulatus, *or Chinese pagoda bush, in full bloom, has grown to tree size in a meadow carpeted with spring flowers at Stourhead, a National Trust property and one of the cradles of landscape design.*

Overleaf: Acid-loving azaleas under a canopy of dogwoods along the Japanese hillside walk at Longwood Gardens in Pennsylvania, an eclectic garden that represents many different styles.

Above: The Chinese Chippendale bridge at Pusey House in Oxfordshire was built in this century.

Below: A stone bridge, which was inspired by an Indian design that features two crouching bulls, crosses a ravine in Sezincote, Gloucestershire. The bridge was built about 1800.

compose, but once the balance is established, it infuses the landscape with a subtle, underlying energy that is lacking in the more static plans of formal gardens. The energy suggests movement, and at the same time, eliminates the boredom of finding a plan that is entirely predictable.

A meandering path is frequently used to connect different settings, or images, in the landscape garden. This emphasis on pictorial image dates back to the eighteenth-century Englishmen who, inspired by the landscape paintings of Poussin and Lorrain, designed gardens as if they were scenes on canvases, with foregrounds, middle grounds, and distant views ordered around focal points such as lakes, temples, or bridges. William Kent, one of the first garden designers to work in the landscape style, was a painter before he became involved in the art of gardening. His plan at Rousham reveals his pictorial technique: the garden begins with a panoramic view across the Cherwell valley, framed by trees and grass, then winds downhill to the river's banks, along a path punctuated by scenic vignettes of pools, statues, a bridge, and a classical temple. Kent's work was naive compared to that of Humphrey Repton, who became the master of the mature landscape style. Repton's landscapes began at the foundation of buildings and stretched gracefully out into the surrounding countryside, emphasizing views rather than vignettes. Yet his approach was also based on painting. In his famous Red Books, he tempted prospective clients with watercolor sketches of their gardens before and after his improvements.

According to Russell Page, Christopher Lloyd, and many other accomplished gardeners, panoramic

Covered in white and blue wisteria is Monet's famous bridge over the lily pond at Giverny. Although he was inspired by a Japanese print, Monet painted the bridge an attractive blue-green color that the Western eye finds more compatible with nature than the vermilion often used in Japan.

Overleaf: Japanese gardens are particularly popular on the West Coast of the United States, which is closer to Japan than any other gardening area of the Western world. Within the Japanese garden at the Huntington Botanical Gardens in San Marino, California, are various kinds of Pinus densiflora, *or Japanese red pine (the multitrunked one is* Pinus densiflora umbraculifera), *azaleas, camellias, flowering peaches, cherries, apricots, and irises and* Acer palmatum, *or Japanese maples. Of equal importance in this setting are the ornaments, stone lanterns, votive stones, and the vermilion-painted bridge —which are essential elements in Japanese temple and shrine architecture.*

The garden at Rousham House is the most definitive example of the landscape style espoused by William Kent. Statues of various Greek gods and goddesses have been used to populate gardens and parks throughout the ages, such as this faun studying a pond.

scenery need not be part of a designed landscape. In fact, many suggest that a good garden and a glorious view are incompatible, that within a composition, foreground and distance should be complementary rather than competitive. Where the view is spectacular, the garden should serve as a simple frame; if the surrounding landscape is plainly unimpressive or if it is not part of the plan, views within the garden can be developed more elaborately, with unusual plants and eye-catching ornaments.

The open spaces within the landscape garden are devoted to water and to grass. Whether still or moving, in lakes, ponds, streams, or brooks, water attracts attention. Extensive landscapes demand large bodies of water; these are often placed in a relatively distant position, where they will not dominate the entire garden plan. Scale and proportion are generous, as landscape designers tend to work with broad exposures, and with bulldozers rather than with spades. Perhaps the most ambitious earth-workers were the eighteenth-century garden makers. They were adept at building dams and managed to harness a number of rivers in the process of creating bodies of water large enough to suit the scale of their clients' immense houses. The lakes at Blenheim and Stourhead, for example, are man-made, and actually were created from small streams.

While water works well in the distance, grass is invaluable in the foreground, exaggerating swells and swales and providing the perfect foil for views. A great expanse of closely cropped lawn is the hallmark of the landscape garden and is the legacy of the eighteenth-century designer Lancelot "Capa-

The main view from Rousham House is calm and Elysian in spirit. Focal points such as a sculpture of a lion attacking a horse are indispensable for providing interest to the landscape.

*D*elicate white wisteria climbs up a railing at Scotney Castle.

bility" Brown. Nicknamed for his keen ability to interpret a site's character or "genius," which he referred to as its "capabilities," Brown reduced his gardens to trees and grass, eliminating flower beds, balustraded parterres, and patterned planting. Brown's taste for simple scenery has continued to influence succeeding generations of gardeners, particularly those in the United States.

If water and lawns create the openings in landscape gardens, it is the masses of trees that define their overall design. Shaping landscape spaces involves clearing trees as often as it includes adding new ones, primarily because carving space out of existing woods is far more efficient than trying to establish enclosures with saplings. Thus the large trees that provide the garden's framework are usually natives, growing in homogeneous clusters of two or three varieties. The specimen trees, on the other hand, are likely to be imported species with certain desirable ornamental qualities, such as their overall shape, or blossoms, or leaves, and as such have a different role to play. Positioning these specimens in the garden is one of the most challenging aspects of landscape gardening. Most often these ornamental trees are set where their silhouettes are clearly visible and where their special features are seen to advantage.

What most clearly reveals that a landscape has been designed is its architectural elements. These structures, which range from bridges and temples to arches, ruins, grottoes, pavilions, follies, teahouses, and gazebos, are the only ornaments in a scenery that otherwise seems untouched by human hands. They provide a clue as to when a particular setting was created. During the eighteenth century, the temples and ruins similar to those that appear on the canvases of Claude Lorrain became desirable features in the landscape gardens seeking Arcadian echoes of the past and paying homage to antiquity. Gradually, classical structures yielded to a more exotic romanticism that found its picturesque expression in Chinese pagodas and Indian bridges, in hermitages and rustic shelters, and in fabricated ruins and crumbling Gothic arches, which presented a comment on the vanity of man's creations and their vulnerability in the face of natural forces. Eventually, the taste for "sublime" beauty developed, with its dramatic emphasis on rugged trees, savage scenery (cliffs and waterfalls), and melancholy moods. Thus, evergreens with somber colors and drooping silhouettes, as well as contorted or pendulous trees such as weeping willows and beeches, were planted to make landscapes look more beautiful. In one garden Humphrey Repton actually erected the cragged trunk of a dead tree. In addition, unusual trees were often set alongside architectural features: cedars of Lebanon were used to complement the massive stone bridge at Blenheim, and Chilean bamboo and Chinese hydrangeas were planted to provide background for the Indian bridge at Sezincote.

Bridges remained a popular feature in landscape gardens. An artifice such as a temple or a miniature pantheon requires a fairly grand scheme and considerable expenditure, but a footbridge needs only a small stream. Moreover, either alone or together with water, bridges always invite attention and provide a striking focal point. Bridges also are often used to adorn peripheral settings, or to delineate the

Above: The Chinese Dairy at Woburn Abbey in Bedfordshire, England, was built during a period of exotic romanticism that flourished near the end of the eighteenth century. Although chinoiserie became popular, China's major contribution to Western horticulture was its mystical enjoyment of landscape rather than its architectural structures such as kiosks and pagodas.

Below: The temple of Ancient Virtue positioned on the Elysian Fields next to the River Styx at Stowe in Buckinghamshire. The principal ornaments in the otherwise understated, all-green landscape gardens of the eighteenth century were Greek and Roman temples and Palladian buildings.

Water tumbles down one of the cascades that connects the eleven ponds in the woodland garden of Mr. and Mrs. Gianni Agnelli at Villar Perosa, near Turin. Designed by Russell Page, it appears completely natural.

Page 242–243: Scotney Castle, in Kent, a National Trust property, has the best-preserved and the most romantic picturesque landscape garden; it was established in 1836 by Edward Hussey. The ruined seventeenth-century villa, with its fourteenth-century tower surrounded by a moat, is enhanced by rhododendrons and various climbers creeping up the old walls.

Preceding overleaf: One of the lily ponds near the subtropical section of the Huntington Gardens in San Marino, California, is bordered by iris and bamboo and surrounded by rare conifers. An unusual landscape garden, it is designed in the classical English fashion, but contains tropical plants.

boundary where the designed plan dissolves and the natural landscape begins. The Chinese Chippendale bridge at Pusey House, for instance, marks passage from the perennial border and flower beds to a wilder landscape that harbors a collection of trees and variegated shrubs.

Even when the link between the designed and the natural landscape is not literally bridged, the transition is usually a smooth one. No explicit boundaries demarcate where the garden ends and the surrounding countryside begins; rather, the cultivated landscape melts almost imperceptibly into its environs. In the eighteenth century, this transition was made possible by an ingenious invention called the ha-ha, a cross between a ditch and a retaining wall that kept cows and sheep from foraging among the plantings near the house. Ha-has are invisible from higher ground, which meant that lawns could continue seemingly unobstructed, creating a simple foreground for distant views. The cattle that grazed in the middle distance, just beyond the ha-ha, were a suitable addition to the pastoral scenery.

As a style, the landscape movement had an astonishing and almost instantaneous success. Innumerable formal gardens were plowed under and replanted as landscapes, not only in Great Britain, but in other European countries too, where *jardins anglais* and *giardini inglesi* attest to the broad appeal of the informally designed garden with its shades of green, its imported trees, and its natural touch.

Nowhere else, however, has the concept of the landscape garden had as much impact as it has had in the United States. It set the pattern for public parks across the nation. Inspired by Kent and Brown, Frederick Law Olmsted, the prominent nineteenth-century landscape architect, converted nearly 800 rocky acres in the middle of Manhattan into a scenically landscaped park. He is still considered America's foremost garden designer, and the numerous urban parks, botanical gardens, shopping centers, and suburban yards designed as natural landscapes rather than cultivated as formal plots bear witness to his influence. Most American gardens consist of trees, shrubs, and lawn casually combined. They are settings rather than gardens, neither complicated to install nor to maintain. That alone probably accounts for much of their practical appeal.

Above: Each of the eleven ponds has its own distinctive plants, such as Cornus kousa chinensis, *on the left.*

Below: A bridge crossing a ravine in the Agnelli garden leads to the wilder parts of the woodland. The work of human hands is clearly visible in the sheared hedge.

X
The Naturalized Garden

*I*ris siberica *is one of the most suitable plants for naturalizing, as it takes care of itself once established.*

*P*age 249: *In the naturalized garden, man's interest focuses on the plant itself, its botanical classification, and its natural requirements. A majestic plant that lends scale and sculptural shape to any setting is the moisture-loving* Gunnera manicata, *with its gigantic leaves and impressive three-foot-high brownish flower spike.*

*P*receding overleaf: *One of America's outstanding contributions to horticulture is the woodland garden at Winterthur, developed by Henry Francis du Pont in 1902. Kurume azaleas and Dexter Hybrid Rhododendrons are among the more exotic plants successfully blended with native dogwoods, ferns, trilliums, bluebells, and mayapples. Among the indigenous trees are beeches, oaks, and tulip poplars.*

*O*pposite: *Dr. Smart's bog garden in Marwood, North Devon, is home to a variety of plants that have adapted to the wet ground. Astilbes (Federsee, Granat, Cologne) can be seen in the foreground, and waving in the wind in the rear are the plumes of* Aruncus sylvester, *or goat's beard. To the right are day lilies and* Salvia uliginosa, *while primulas and linarias are sprinkled throughout.*

*D*istinct garden styles evolve in response to such factors as personal taste, the character of the land, the constraints of time, money, space, and climate. Today, the relationship between man and nature is a rational one, inspired by science rather than romance, and the style that has developed as a result is the naturalized garden. Admired for its genuine simplicity and lack of contrivance, the naturalized garden has plants as its primary ingredient, arranged according to natural rather than formal principles. Drifts, groves, and glades take the place of beds, borders, and architectural elements. Yet no matter how random the planting may appear, it is designed with a picture in mind.

The twentieth-century approach to gardening translates into a willingness to work within the framework of the site—be it existing meadows or marshes, woodlands or watery bogs—and with the features of the natural environment. It involves a process of elaboration rather than elimination, of intensifying the original features and then melding the cultivated area into the surrounding landscape. Thus, designing a naturalized garden is not a purely aesthetic exercise of selecting a favorite style and applying it to the site—it is an undertaking that involves analysis and environmental sensitivity as well as artistic ability.

Ideally, the plants that make up the naturalized garden should be so well adapted to the local conditions that they will multiply prolifically and ultimately, will create a self-sufficient landscape that blooms and fades with minimal attention from the resident gardener. They need not all be native, however. Exotics are acceptable as long

The Desert Garden at Huntington Gardens in San Marino, California, is unique because of its approximately 2,000 varieties of succulents—trees and shrubs that survive by storing water in their thick stems or leaves. Echinocereos cinerascens *has pink blossoms. On the left rises the upright column of* Borzicactus celsianus *from Bolivia; in the middle is* Opuntia phaecantha major *from North America; and in the background on the right is* Agava salmiana.

Preceding overleaf:
Since Monet's time, gardeners have favored planting monochromatic groups of strong-colored flowers. The late William Suhr, in his woodland garden in Westchester, massed together azaleas in various shades of red and white. These shrubs thrive in the acidic soils of the East Coast.

as they can survive and prosper on the site. Both plan and planting are loosely informal and so closely modeled upon the landscape's original features that they appear undesigned.

A reverence for nature, which is fundamental to this style of garden design, has been deeply ingrained in the twentieth-century consciousness. In the United States, the wilderness has played a dominant role in shaping the nation. From seventeenth-century Pilgrims to nineteenth-century pioneers and prospectors, Americans have had to contend with untamed landscapes. Henry David Thoreau, inspired by the woods of Massachusetts, and John Muir by those of California, philosophized about nature's healthy influence and inspiration. In addition to being national heroes, George Washington and Thomas Jefferson were actively involved in creating their own gardens, while Theodore Roosevelt, who loved the outdoors, created five national parks during his presidency. Many of their counterparts today are occupied with ecological concerns on another scale. And authors such as Rachel Carson and Stephen Jay Gould attempt to stimulate reverence and environmental awareness by bringing a more detailed picture of nature and natural processes to the attention of the American public.

An appreciation of nature, of course, is not exclusive to the United States. It is a universal phenomenon that has its intellectual origins in the eighteenth century when Jean Jacques Rousseau, the French philosopher and writer, embraced all that was natural and chastised all that was not. He praised nature as innately good and condemned society as inherently corrupt. In addressing the relationship

Chorisia speciosa, *or
the pink silk-floss tree, stores water in its
trunk, which is protected by thorns. It is
surrounded by kalanchoes: the yellow flowers
on the left are grandiflora, from India; and
the pink blooms on the right are* Kalanchoes
fedtschenkoi, *from Madagascar. The tree
on the left is an* Aloe candelabrum.

Above: At the Huntington Desert Garden, winter blooms are provided by succulents of African origin; spring and summer color is supplied by cacti and other American plants.

Below: A barrel cactus rises out of a sea of blue Senecio mandraliscae. The red blooms belong to aloes.

Opposite: The snake-like cactus Trichocereus thelegonus originated in Argentina.

between man and nature, Rousseau originally advocated gardens grown informally, but by the end of his life, his approach was more radical. Ultimately, he rejected the art of gardening altogether, convinced that in cultivating pleasure grounds, man was disfiguring nature.

The eighteenth-century Romantics and the Picturesque movement that they inspired fostered an appreciation for "improved" nature. Bernardin de St.-Pierre, who endorsed Rousseau's exaltation of nature, augmented it when he wrote a treatise on gardens in which he extolled the introduction of exoticism and the use of tropical plants in temperate zones. Today, his statue stands proudly in the Jardin des Plantes in Paris, and the exoticism that he advanced is what subtly differentiates naturalized gardens from the uncultivated landscapes that surround them. Stands of bamboo, a deep purple cotinus, a lush-looking fatsia, or the large, lacy leaves of ailanthus interspersed with oaks and maples in a twentieth-century garden pay homage to him.

If St.-Pierre succeeded in whetting our appetites for exotica, plant hunters provided the nourishment, venturing to the far corners of the world in search of trees, shrubs, bulbs, and any plant that might be coaxed to grow in their gardens at home. During the nineteenth century, numerous adventurers traveled to the Far East and brought back a wealth of Oriental plants. E. H. Wilson returned with Chinese species and Charles Sprague Sargent introduced many of the botanical riches of Japan to the U.S. by way of Harvard's Arnold Arboretum. As a result, naturalizers today are endowed with a plentiful repertoire of plants gathered

Columnar golden cacti, golden barrel cacti, African aloes, and a giant South American cereus compete for space at the Huntington Desert Garden.

Opposite: The Hortense Miller garden in Laguna Beach is full of indigenous Californian and drought-resistant Australian plants that have a chance of surviving the fires that often sweep through the canyon. Agaves, artemisias, iceflowers, nasturtiums, and native wild flowers turn what was a desert into a flowering hillside.

from places that are distant geographically but essentially alike ecologically. Thus, a cultivated woodland in New England hosts azaleas native to the mountains of eastern Japan; a seashore garden in California burgeons with hardy material from Asia; and gardens like the Fentons', also in California, support collections of gray-leaved plants that are Mediterranean in origin and therefore well-adapted to heat and drought.

In terms of style, naturalized gardening owes a debt to both eighteenth-century designed landscapes and the late-nineteenth- and early-twentieth-century English flower gardens. From the landscape school it has taken an emphasis on the pictorial and the perception of the garden as part of the surrounding countryside. Woodland gardens such as the one at Winterthur, in Delaware, for instance, are shaped according to eighteenth-century standards, with dogwood and rhododendron grouped in groves and around glades cut from a canopy of larger native trees. Virtually all evidence of man has been either camouflaged or removed—a trend that was launched with the landscape school and then taken a step further by the naturalizers. Masonry walls, terraces, ornate flights of steps, and sculpted deities are gone; only a footpath and an occasional bench remain.

Borrowed from the English style is the notion of the garden as a snug harbor—a place that protects a wide range of different plants. And as in the best English schemes, a naturalized garden is a plant collector's haven. But the selection of plants in a naturalized garden is subject to the specific limitations of the site. Whether it is high land or low, a beech wood or a winding

brook, the natural environment and its conditions dictate which species will grow and which will not. The cactus section at the Huntington Botanical Garden, for example, is an extreme environment—sunny, hot, and dry. It is suited only to succulents and cacti, for no thin-skinned woodland plants would survive. A wetland, on the other hand, invites irises and astilbes, sedges, and arum lilies, and relegates dry-loving cinquefoils and sedums to troughs. The resulting limitation is a boon to plant lovers, for they are an acquisitive lot by nature, and acquisition is an additive process that is often at odds with order.

The inherent compatability between plant and place has ensured that naturalized gardens require little maintenance. The Hortense Miller garden, set on the steep slopes of a canyon in southern California, is an extreme illustration —even the periodic brush fires that sweep through are considered part of the local ecology, and the plants in the most exposed sections are species that have adapted to an occasional burning. In any environment, the ultimate goal of naturalizing is to foster a population of plants that will thrive with minimal attention: a mass of daffodils provides a straightforward example for they bloom year after year once established and demand only an occasional afternoon spent dividing bulbs and distributing them farther afield.

The carefree quality of gardening naturalistically is further underlined by the fact that change is built into the naturalizing process; for once in the ground, plants are given free rein to establish and extend themselves as best they can. As populations shift and concentrations change, the savvy gardener

*F*erns are among the
most useful of plants because they thrive in
moist shady sites and can be used as ground
cover. Although flowerless, they are graceful
and delicate in appearance. Many different
species grow in North America, which is
unusually rich in ferns.

Santolinas, lavender, oleander bushes, and olive trees populate Mr. and Mrs. Howard Fenton's garden in the hills of Santa Barbara, California. Mediterranean plants thrive in this climate, which is similar to that of their origin; the daffodil, on the other hand, needed to be refrigerated for a while before it could bloom.

cultivates a cavalier attitude about what grows where. Christopher Lloyd's garden at Great Dixter in Sussex is an extraordinary combination of structured rooms and swatches of naturalized ground. In one section, for instance, a band of fritillaria originally scattered along the top of a bank has prospered, and as the bulbs have multiplied, they gradually have gravitated downhill. In spring, the entire slope is a sheet of bloom; even the stream bed below, which was originally too damp for flowers, is filled with fritillaria. Such changes are welcome in naturalizing; but they demand supervision if the line between naturalized and natural is to be maintained. The moment gardeners turn their backs, nature sets to work to reclaim her turf, transforming beds to briar patches and fields to forests.

Plants are paramount in the naturalized garden, as they are in the English garden. The main difference between the two styles is that the plants in an English garden are organized within a clearly articulated framework, while there is no such formal order in the naturalized. The plants most admired by naturalizers are the tough, free-spirited species. Bulbs are particularly prized for, once comfortably established, they are generous dividers. Self-seeders are also favored, as is any plant with seeds that appeal to foraging fauna, because it is guaranteed good distribution. Plants that need pampering are not so successful, although a devoted gardener can always find room for one or two choice but less stalwart selections.

"To be fair," wrote turn-of-the-century landscape architect Charles Eliot, "it must be fit," and although his words apply to many different styles and situations, they

Christopher Lloyd pays great attention to the meadows in and around his garden at Great Dixter. A meadow under a hawthorn tree is found within the garden, near the entrance.

A field of Amaryllis hippeastrum *grows in the subtropical section of the Huntington Gardens in San Marino, California. When planted outdoors, these bulbous plants flower freely and retain their evergreen leaves, provided the climate is similar to their native South African habitat.*

are particularly appropriate to the naturalized garden, for compatibility between the site and the planting is the primary goal. The horticultural fit assures a visual fit: plants that survive in a specific niche look right because they have evolved in that environment and have adapted the appropriate color, size, and shape. The overall effect is much more subtle, however. Wild flowers, for example, are more ephemeral than the hybrid flowers that are bred for beds. Their colors tend to be soft and their blossoms are often small, but they "fit" in fields and meadows, and therein lies the source of their beauty. In other garden styles, beauty depends largely upon order imposed by man; with naturalization that relationship is reversed. Applied artistry is reduced to a minimum and nature is encouraged to shine on its own. For the gardener who works in this style, every plot of land contains the seed of a potential garden.

Naturalized gardens do not consist entirely of flowers and herbaceous plants. Shapely trees and shrubs offer great variety and will prove rewarding additions, especially during the bleak months of winter. Evergreens are often used to create a strong backbone, and deciduous species that retain their withered leaves can be relied on to arouse interest. This style has also encouraged some new tastes. Many species of ornamental grasses, for instance, are admired for precisely those qualities for which they were formerly spurned: they are tenacious, and in winter their tussocks of golden leaves are now considered an asset rather than an untidy habit. Seed pods, stalks, and dried leaves that were once snipped because they were considered unsightly are now left in place and

The bog garden at Marwood in Devon is rich in irises and primulas; pampas grass adds an exotic note.

*The mayapple (*Podo-phyllum peltatum*) is one of the many American wild flowers that carpets rich woodland areas. It blooms in May, and dies to the ground by summer.*

Opposite: The Cypress Gardens in Charleston, South Carolina, were once the site of a reservoir used for holding water that would later be released to flood the fields on the Dean Hall rice plantation. In 1927, the native forest of bald cypress trees was turned into a water garden with the addition of Indian and kurume azaleas and drifts of daffodils. Today, it can be visited by boat. Taxodium distichum, or bald cypress, is a deciduous conifer, native to the southeastern United States and a relative of the California dawn redwood. It grows to a height of 150 feet and can live 1,000 years.

admired as ornamental.

To attribute the naturalized garden's success entirely to its ease of maintenance would be a mistake, however. It also has strong intellectual and emotional appeal. Specifically, the naturalized garden responds to the twentieth-century gardener's ecological awareness and sense of responsibility as a steward for the environment. Moreover, it reflects contemporary social inclinations. The naturalized garden is a popular approach because it is fundamentally democratic. The naturalized garden does not depend upon the impressive exhibitions of power and control that the French garden was designed for; nor does it set out to dazzle its audience with displays of horticultural virtuosity. As a style, the naturalized garden is especially appropriate for the millions of gardeners in the United States, for it is applicable in a wide range of environments, from the mountains of Maine to the California desert. Vast acreage and endless capital are not essential, although a naturalized garden can be extraordinarily lavish, with extensive grounds full of rare and unusual plants. Even in the extreme, the naturalized garden is never an overtly ostentatious style.

Acknowledgments

I would like to express my gratitude to:

Tessa Traeger, without whom this book would not have been begun or finished.

Mr. and Mrs. Gianni Agnelli, for taking an interest in and supporting my photographic endeavors.

House & Garden and its editors and art directors, who pushed me in the right direction.

My children, Tom and Cady, for having demonstrated patience and understanding toward a working mother.

The gardeners who provided the true substance of this book.

M.S.

With thanks to John and Marybeth Weston, who made it possible.

S.L.

Index

Design

J. C. Suarès

Kathleen Gates
Michelle Siegel

Production

Katherine van Kessel
Carol Chien

Composed in Caslon 540
by U.S. Lithograph Inc.,
New York, New York
Printed and bound
by Toppan Printing Company, Ltd.,
Tokyo, Japan